*To Our Friends
at Sun America —*

THE
WISDOM
OF OUR
BURDENS

A fable

Volume I

From Debt to Deliverance

RUTH
THEOBALD PROBST

Ruth Theobald Probst

LifeMark Press
Celebrating the brilliance of each human spirit

THE WISDOM OF OUR BURDENS
Volume I
From Debt to Deliverance

For information or to order additional copies please contact
LifeMark Press
a division of
LifeMark Institute for Greatness, LLC
21150 W. Capitol Drive, Suite 3, Pewaukee, WI 53072
Toll-free 877-783-1133

For information on other works by Ruth Theobald Probst,
or her workshops, book signing and speaking events,
or to invite her to speak to your group, please visit her website
www.wisdomofourburdens.com

ISBN 0-9753422-0-7

Printed in the United States
10 9 8 7 6 5 4 3 2 1

Dedication

This book is dedicated
to you, the reader.

May you find
the wisdom of your own burdens
and revel in the wonder of who you are.

Foreword

Many stories are told. Few stories have a lasting impression. In this story, you will meet a unique woman who will dramatically change your perceptions of the world and of yourself. Avery Victoria Spencer is a successful business woman who through her life's journey learns the difference between material wealth and spiritual wealth. Avery will intrigue, provoke, and inspire you with her views on money, joy, responsibility, choice, and inner wisdom. Her ideas will encourage you to view your own burdens as gifts. Her story will challenge you emotionally, psychologically, and spiritually. You will be transformed by the characters in this story and the messages they bring. Throughout the chapters of this story, you will be invited to discover the wisdom of your 'essential' burdens and find your 'greatness.'

From the beginning of civilization, humans have struggled with the question, "What is my purpose in life?" The author,

Ruth Theobald Probst, answers this question simply and profoundly. One's purpose is to be true to oneself and to make choices out of love rather than fear. To live an authentic life is to achieve 'greatness.' To be positive about life's experiences, even its burdens, is to achieve spiritual growth. To rely on one's intuition rather than past negative messages is to achieve emotional and psychological freedom.

In my private practice as a psychologist, I have found that humans suffering from depression and/or anxiety have no meaning in life. They have a negative view of themselves, a negative view of the world, and a negative view of the future. Depressed individuals have learned to send negative messages to themselves. Examples of these messages are: "I am a failure. Things will never change. The world is a cruel place." When individuals change the message, they change the feeling which then leads to a behavioral change. This is the foundation of cognitive therapy.

In this book, Avery changes her negative messages and finds her authentic and real self. She starts to live from a place that she chooses rather than one that others in her past have chosen for her. She views her burdens especially with money from a different perspective—a positive perspective from which to learn and gather inner wisdom. She learns to make choices out of love rather than out of fear. She learns to trust her inner voice.

In my work as a nurse, I have found that humans can use their pain and suffering, their burdens, as powerful pathways to change their lives for the better. Ruth's story illustrates the transformation that can occur when one embraces life's burdens as gifts. Her story will encourage you to do the same.

During the time Ruth was writing her story, I was diagnosed with breast cancer. I asked myself what could I learn about life and what could I learn about myself through this burden. I certainly did not embrace cancer as a gift. Then I remembered Ruth's story. I used the experience of pain and suffering to help clarify my values, to sort out what matters to me most and what doesn't. My burden became a gift. The gift was love from my family, friends, and colleagues. I found out how much people really love me. I had gained the wisdom of my burden.

Although this book is fiction, it represents Ruth's search for meaning in her life. She relates 'the only way to true fulfillment and purpose is by listening to and honoring your own inner wisdom.' I admire and respect Ruth for her journey. It has been long and arduous. I have watched Ruth heal from her past, live in her present, and embrace her future. She has achieved inner wisdom, spiritual growth, and freedom to be herself. She has discovered that she is a special person, full of wisdom, courage, grace, and greatness. In her enthusiasm and zeal, she has wanted to share her journey through this story. My life has been enriched by her story. May your life by enriched. May you find your inner wisdom.

Joyce M. Wallskog, RN, PhD
Clinical Assistant Professor of Nursing,
Marquette University–Milwaukee, WI
Licensed Psychologist
Advanced Practice Nurse Prescriber

Introduction

This is a fable. It is also the story of a journey inward, prompted by a desperate need to know an answer I could not get from any other source. I never knew that a story could save me; I did not know that a story could take me to a place of profound inner wisdom that would change my life. So while this is very much my own story, it is not just my own. For the story has been given to me, I believe, as a gift to be shared with others. That much has been clear from the start.

For most of my life, I carried a heavy burden of financial woe. I had been poor and not poor; had money, not had it, then had it again. My relationship with money was complicated and unhappy. We were strange bedfellows, my money and I, always awkward with each other and uncomfortable. Certainly never intimate.

During the years of my life that were dedicated to religious service, I was to 'trust God' for everything, which really meant that our family relied on the generosity of others for support.

Completely. Much of that time we learned to do without, sometimes to the point of empty cupboards and stomachs. We did not starve, but I had the sense that God was withholding; that somehow we were being punished for a lack of faith and commitment. There was never enough money.

Breaking away at last from a life for which I had been trained but to which my heart did not belong, I found myself thrust into a secular society that not only did I not understand, but which I had been taught to abhor.

I began on Abraham Maslow's lowest rung in the "Hierarchy of Needs"—survival. Money was the most basic tool and I learned to earn. I gave myself completely to the task and found I rather enjoyed the challenge. I was actually good at it. I began to make money. And more money—finally to the point where I was earning what only three percent of women in this prosperous country have accomplished. But still there was never enough.

My relationship with money did not improve as my income increased. I could make money, but could not save it... could not stand to have it in my life for long. The more I made, the more I spent. As I became more financially successful, my debt load increased. The burden of my financial woes simply got heavier until I could bear it no longer.

Over the course of time, I had done many things to attempt to resolve this problem, but they had all failed miserably. I had read and studied about money and prosperity. Even today my library contains volumes of well-written, articulate books about money. I tried this approach and that technique, various budgets, and strict record keeping. I sought financial counseling. The only thing these attempts did was make me more aware of how inept I was. Nothing I tried did anything to resolve my problem.

Reaching my wits' end, I lay in bed one evening (March 10, 2000, to be exact) and wondered, "What if I could speak to my financial burden—to 'that which I cannot overcome,'" as I had learned to call it. What would it say? It was in a dream that night that this fable began.

The startling lesson I learned as I was given this story was that the answer lies within us. Those things that we cannot overcome, no matter what we do, are meant to draw us to the wisdom that cannot be found anywhere but in the recesses of our own inner knowing. We each have challenges in life that we ache to overcome... burdens that we carry because, try as we might, we cannot unshackle them. These are 'essential' burdens because they are intended to teach us what we need to know in order to live our lives more fully and authentically. They will not leave us until their mission is accomplished.

'Essential' burdens are gifts. They beg to take us to the next level of the experience of life, to teach us more, and ultimately to show us our own wonder, goodness, and greatness. Our own wisdom. Each challenge we face, each burden we carry, is an invitation to reach higher by going deeper into ourselves. As Neale Donald Walsh writes in *Conversations with God*, "All things lead us to our innermost truth. That is their purpose."

What I share with you now is the story I was given on my journey within. What I learned as a result of that adventure has profoundly changed my life. In the process, my financial burden has been lifted.

This story is not about forsaking the assistance of others as we face our particular challenges. Many of our problems can be resolved by the wisdom and knowledge we glean from their insights. But we cannot expect to lay our 'essential burdens' at the feet of another and be healed. This story is about learning to recognize that all true healing requires us to go within ourselves. It is about the serendipitous beginning of being at our wits' end.

It is my hope that in the reading of this fable you will be drawn to that place of wisdom within yourself and the wonder it holds for you.

May you revel in the adventure that awaits you.

Ruth Theobald Probst
2004

The Light and the Darkness

Anything that draws you into your own wisdom
Is Light;
Anything that distracts you from its discovery
Is Darkness.

If you believe a technique, a method,
a belief system, a pill, another person is
Your Light…
If you believe something outside of you
has the key to your life, you live in
Your Darkness.

The wisdom you crave lies within you;
accept only that which guides you to your
Own Light.
You may glean wisdom from others,
but only your own light can penetrate your
Own Darkness.

Accept the gift of light from others; but do not walk in others' shadows.

Their Light is not Your Light.

They carry their own burdens;

Their Darkness is not Your Darkness.

The wisdom of your burdens draws you to your
Unique Light.

Their true purpose is to dissolve your
Unique Darkness.

Be the Light!

Own the Light!

Live the Light!

Let the light of your unique brilliance shine.

It is who you are.

Ruth L. Theobald Probst
October 5, 2003

Prologue

A doorbell. I hear a doorbell. How can that be? There are no doorbells in medieval castles—no telephones, no computers declaring that I have mail, no electricity, and certainly no plumbing. No clocks, clicking off the precious minutes of life. I love that. I have learned to cherish being here. It's my own castle, which you can plainly see by the coat of arms that appears everywhere. While I was most reluctant to come here, now it is home. In spite of its cold stone surfaces and interminable chill, its rough walls, and poor lighting. I love it. Even the lack of plumbing doesn't bother me.

But the sound of the doorbell does. I hear it again. It means I have returned to that insidious dimension of time and space called 'today.' To doorbells and electricity, cell phones and computers, not to mention the latest technological advances brought to us by the internet: e-mails, instant messaging, and palm pilots. And to clocks, ticking away the seconds of life, causing hurry and worry. Oh, dreary, demanding life. Yes, plumbing is an advantage, but not enough to interest me in returning. Willing my eyes to remain closed, I focus on my breathing so that I can pretend I have not left the castle—the place of my awakening.

There is a certain peace in the inefficiencies of castle life. They allow one to slow down to a different pace, especially when one is alone and chained in a dungeon. Oh yes, that was the best thing that ever happened to me. To have to do nothing. Life becomes only the rhythm of breathing. There is only this moment, only this inhale, only this exhale. I know I shall miss it—even the chains in the dungeon where I was a prisoner. Even those.

For it was there that I learned to love the quiet, the solitude, and the absence of distraction. I learned to breathe into and become my own true self. Yes, I knew from the beginning that I would return here to today. In fact, I can remember being intently focused on how to get back to this dimension, but just in the beginning. Because I was afraid I might not be able to come back. HA! What I wouldn't give now for just one more moment there in that timeless place. "Please," I beg. "Let me remember that place; the transformational journey. Every detail." I pause. Inhale... exhale.

The doorbell chimes again, only louder now. I smile in spite of myself. For in the chiming is the answer to my request to linger in the castle. The answer, as clear as it ever was in the castle. It is time to be here again. The familiar sound of the Westminster chimes of the doorbell of my own home declare "Welcome home, Avery Victoria Spencer." Welcome home indeed.

Yes, I have returned. And whether time stood still while I took this incredible journey or whether in my return to this lower, limited dimension of time and space, hours, days, or years have passed, I do not know. Nor do I care. For I will never be the same.

I am not who I was when I lay down to nap back 'before'—whenever that was—trying to avoid dealing with my financial woes, ending up in the castle where I met my own self and my own wisdom; where my financial woes were healed in the most startling way. I have visited a place inside of me that I never knew existed. A place of such wonder and such wisdom that I know my own self in a new and glorious way.

The doorbell again. Reluctant but curious, I open my eyes and the room comes into view. It is the sunroom of my own rather opulent home, the place where I had lain down so despondently after opening my mail and facing the reality of my financial crisis once again. So long ago it seems. I close my eyes once more, aching to recapture the last scene of the incredible dream. I will never forget any of it, and yet, I want to capture it again; one more time in my mind's eye.

There it is... the room in which the woman was writing the ending to a beautiful story. And then she became me and I was writing.

Yes, I remembered. I would write this story. That's how I would keep the memory alive in my heart. Suddenly it was good to be home. Now that I knew I did not really have to leave where I had been. That place, that story was inside of me. I would bring it to life again by writing.

The doorbell rings again and I become more conscious of my surroundings. As I look about me, I realize that this house doesn't feel right. Yes, it is my home, but it is different somehow. Too big? Overly decorated? Foreign at least. Not mine. Do I really live here? I recognize everything, but still it feels strangely uncomfortable.

I pull myself up to a sitting position and drag my legs over the edge of the sofa and on to the floor. The plush carpet under my feet shocks my senses. I had acclimated so well to cold stone floors that this cushion under my feet feels strange. It unbalances me. It's as if I am visiting another country. In fact, that's exactly how I feel right now... like a stranger in a strange land. What used to be familiar to me is no longer.

The doorbell again. Oh, bother.

Standing is not easy. The room lurches around me and I have to fight for my balance. My body has returned to this room, but part of me, including my equilibrium, is still in transit. I am secretly glad. It reassures me that I was truly there and not here. That is what makes me glad.

Steadying myself against the wicker sofa, I take a step forward. Wobbly but still upright, I congratulate myself on my success. Steady, easy. Good. And now, another. Slowly. Carefully. OK, I remember how to do this walking on carpet. I inch forward toward the kitchen where I know the firm floor will greet me and take me to the door. I don't feel weak, just unsteady, and unsure.

I reach the kitchen and my feet are glad of the certainty of the stone floor. Glancing at the counter I see the stack of overdue bills as I had left them. How can I describe my new-found attitude toward them? Can one be overjoyed to see bills that they cannot pay? YES! They have taught me so much. They are what took me on this incredible journey that feels so very real that I will never forget it. I smile lovingly at them and keep walking toward the door. For I know that even at this moment my financial issues are resolved. They have taught me; I have listened to their message and now they will simply and quietly disappear, just like the spirit guides I met in the castle.

The doorbell sounds once again as if to remind me to continue. Everything feels surreal, like this is a dream and that my life in the castle was reality. Finally I am at the front door.

Ugh. I do not want to see anyone just yet. I will whoever it is to be gone and as I look through the peek hole, it appears that no one is there. I check myself over in the mirror to the right of the foyer just in case. Staring back at me is a radiant, beautiful woman. It is me, still dressed in my tailored white shirt and jeans. The woman in the mirror is smiling, but more than that, she is glowing from somewhere inside. It's my eyes that I notice the most. They simply sparkle in a way they have not before. I am beautiful from within.

The doorbell rings again, this time with an attitude. I don't even think to question how that can be done when no one appears to be outside. I have just come from a place where strange and incredible events are normal occurrences. In fact, I do not even consider this as anything unusual.

I open the door. Seeing no one, I step out into the quiet of the day and stumble over something at my feet. I look down to see what has caused the problem. It is a small package. It has no name on it... nothing to suggest that it is mine. But it is here and someone certainly wanted me to know that. Puzzled I reach for it, and feel the shape of it. I have always been good at guessing what is inside a package. This is most certainly a book.

Since I have ordered no books recently, I cannot understand why one has arrived. I pick it up and turn it over looking for the customary mailing label to identify its origin.

My heart stops—then starts beating wildly with awe and joy. For on the back, the flap is secured with a purple wax seal. There is no mistaking the symbol on the seal. It is the coat of arms from the castle. My coat of arms, my castle. Can it be that something real has reached me from that other dimension?

I hug the package to me and quickly step back into the house, shutting the door behind me. I don't want anyone else to see what I think I am about to discover. I move back into the kitchen where my favorite letter opener sits just where it was when I was slitting open the envelopes of my bills. I pick it up and can't help but hesitate a moment before I begin the sacred act of opening this envelope. Inhale. Exhale.

Very gently, I move the letter opener under the seal. I do not want to destroy it. It is still quite soft and pliable which means it was only recently that the candle was lit, the wax dripped in place, and the seal embossed into the hot wax. Executing the opening with the exacting care of a surgeon, I ache to see what is inside. This is another miracle. I used to believe that things like this just didn't happen to sensible people like me. But I now know otherwise in a way I never knew before. Miracles have become a way of life.

I lift the flap and reach inside to remove the contents. I can feel the soft leather. Yes, it is a book. But what book, and how did it get here?

Pulling the soft brown leather book out of the package, I open it and see pages of writing. I recognize the beautiful script; the penmanship is unmistakable. Turning immediately to the last few pages, the only ones that I saw in that last room in the castle, I see those same words. And yes, they are exactly the words that were written there... in that other world—that other world that lives inside of me. That place of profound love and wisdom. The place where I learned how to heal my financial woes but so much more that that. It is the place where I found myself—where I learned that my real problem was not with money, but something much, much more important.

I know that the story has been written in my heart, authored by my very own soul. There is nothing for me to do now, except to revel in it. I have become quite good at reveling. I notice that tears of joy are falling. I have also become quite good at crying tears of joy—joy that I never would have experienced—tears that I would never have let myself cry—before.

There is nothing now that I want to do more than relive those amazing experiences in the castle. I think about making my way back into the sunroom to settle myself into the wicker rocker (which matches the wicker sofa, of course), to begin reading. Then I feel the cold stone surface of the kitchen floor. Much better. Familiar. I settle myself down and open the book.

Avery Victoria Spencer

Chapter 1

The last thing I remember was lying down on the soft floral cushions of my wicker sofa, trying to give in to the relaxing effects of a third generous glass of my favorite Chardonnay while worrying about my never-ending financial troubles.

So, what was I doing here, standing inside what appeared to be an immense, old stone castle? Glancing down at myself, I was slightly relieved to see that I was still dressed in the same attire as when I had lain down—jeans, untucked oxford cloth shirt (which my best friend, Evelyn, had told me would make my inherited ample hips and thighs look thin and lithe), and tennis shoes.

It was cold and damp, about as inviting as stepping into a wet swimsuit. Looking up, I saw blazing torches that taunted me from their lofty positions in the room, which was at least two stories high. With two on each wall, they provided only a modest amount of light, and did nothing to penetrate the chill. Heat rises, of course. I knew that. And its chances of reaching down to me, a mere five feet five inches from the floor, was a scientific impossibility.

1

On one wall, there was a small, high window that told me it was night, since no light was shining through its iron lattices. While it looked like a possible escape route in the event of an emergency, there were two issues I could not overcome. First of all, it was inaccessible; secondly, as I studied the size of the opening against my physique, it was obvious that getting me through the opening was about as likely as getting the mythically 'super-sized' Santa down a fireplace chimney.

Shivering, I rubbed my crossed arms vigorously, wishing I had a sweater or jacket. It didn't help that I could see the fog of my own breath in front of me every time I exhaled. Never one to be caught unprepared, I made a note to myself: the next time you lie down for a nap, Avery Victoria Spencer, wear a sweater and wrap yourself in an afghan, just in case. Oh, yes, and add a pair of socks, warmer shoes, hat, mittens, and, ah, long underwear. Perfect.

I am the president of a small midwestern city bank—practical, level headed, and unemotional. My gift for numbers was obvious at an early age, and my family always assumed that I would end up in a financially related profession. I wore numbers around me like a cloak because only they made me feel warm and secure. I felt that if I could understand numbers, I could control my destiny.

Actually, as a child, I had loved anything that could be put together: not only numbers, but puzzles, Tinker Toys, Lincoln Logs, Erector Sets, you name it—anything that I could put together, take apart, and reassemble into something different. Many of the things I played with are regrettably no longer legal for children under certain ages to handle lest they decide to eat them or stick them where they do not belong. I was lucky to have been born before such limitations were imposed. And my parents had always encouraged my aspirations. I loved them for that.

I was also fascinated by stories and became an avid reader, probably because my mother read to me nightly until I could read for myself. It amazed me the way writers took certain words from all the words in the English language and formed them into stories that could make me laugh, cry, or lie awake terrified. Music held me under the same spell, because someone could put the notes together in a way that was beautiful to hear.

'Gifted' is what they called me. I could have chosen any number of careers—so said all of my teachers. I could have been a scientist, an architect, a writer, a composer, a mathematician...

But all the fun had ended when I went to school. At first, I believed everyone was just like me. It didn't take long to realize that I was different. That being 'gifted' was not a good thing at all. It meant that I was always alone. If that was my 'gift,' I wanted nothing to do with it. It meant that I was unsafe in my small world. The other children played; I studied. They made friends; I had only my imagination as a friend. Being the only child of aged parents who could not understand the world that I lived in did not help.

And to make things worse, I was shy and an only child. I looked with longing at the others in my classes. They laughed and played together, had sleepovers in each other's homes and birthday parties with lots of presents from everyone. Shared secrets on the playground. Passed notes and got in trouble together in school. Flirted with boys, wore the latest fashions. I was an island. And there was no bridge to their world. Trust me, if I had been able to build one, I would have.

And so in my finite world, I put aside the love of everything that required creative imagination, everything from childhood that spoke of being different in some way. I wanted only to be like the other children. I wanted to stop dreaming and seeing the world differently. And I really tried. I stopped putting my hand up in class. I gave up singing and writing stories. I tried to act like everyone else, so that in the end, I never did really create anything at all. And I still didn't have friends.

I figured out that if I had money, I would be accepted. That was the way the world seemed to work. Only money could make me feel safe. If I could not be a part of the world where everyone else seemed to live, I would make money and buy my way in. If poverty was how I grew up, then money would be how I would prove to the world that I was valuable.

I liked numbers, so money concepts came easily to me. Working with money meant working with numbers. Surely if I did something that was involved with money, I would be safe and secure for the rest of my life. And people would look up to me and like me. So with a double major in business management and finance, I decided to take on the banking industry. Everyone, including me, expected me to go far.

But it took much longer than I had anticipated. I learned the money aspects of banking quickly, but it took me years to learn the psychology and political underpinnings of the industry. They didn't teach that in college. They just expected you to know them, which most men apparently did. (I just figured there was a secret society that women weren't invited to join.) As a woman in a predominantly male world, you just either figured it out on your own or... you didn't. And you rose in the ranks (or not) accordingly.

I loved the challenge and slowly but steadily secured higher positions, although my head still bears the scars of crashing against the 'glass ceiling.' I learned to play the game, but as a woman, I learned to play it so subtly that no one noticed what I was up to. Cool-headed, determined, and damn good with numbers, it was an irresistible combination and would have landed a man into the bank president's position years ago.

But here I was, too many years after I began my quest, finally earning the big office at the bank. The one people walked by and peeked into shyly as if there were something sacred about the president's lair. And everyone wanted to say he or she knew me. It was just as I had planned. I was one of the lucky ones. Not many women made it this far. At least that had been my life up to the moment I showed up here, in this uninviting, medieval castle.

Chapter ii

As if on cue, the bank president in me took over and began to coolly and unemotionally assess my situation. My first thought was to create my exit strategy. Just like any bank investment that had taken an unexpected turn, I knew that I could not change the circumstances that had brought me here, but I sure as heck could look for the way out. A puzzle to solve. I would rise to the occasion, I was certain of that.

Finding the back door out of a situation was as natural to me as breathing, thanks to my childhood fascinations and my chosen profession. My natural inclination for taking things apart and putting them back together in different ways made this castle feel like a game of sorts, a challenge.

I lived for challenges, which is why I was so successful with investments, even those that failed to perform to the amazing promises in the prospectus. Most of the deals I did exceeded the investors' expectations. For the ones that didn't, there was no mistake that couldn't be fixed or recast into a new strategic plan. I had several in my repertoire. My attention to detail, blended with honesty and good old-fashioned sweetness, was an unbeatable recipe for success.

Every deal, every investment had to have a way out on the way in. That was how I operated. I knew every nook, crevice, and cliff edge in the deals I did, and I had a 'what if' strategy for each of them. I was very good. I had to be.

So began my quest to find the 'exit strategy' to this castle. I implemented 'Exit Strategy Plan A: Consider the Obvious.' Sometimes the solution was so simple that it was overlooked because it was too easy. I looked around the room. I knew the one window I had seen was not an option. Even with a ladder, I would be unable to fit through the opening, not to speak of the drop I may have to make on the other side, which would probably kill me. I felt around the cold stone walls for any movement that might be an invisible door. Nothing. I looked around for any tools to hammer my way out. Hell, I'd even make do with a large rock. Anything. That was the banker in me again—create an exit if one didn't already exist.

But there was no obvious means of escape. "OK, keep cool, Avery Victoria," I said to myself. "'Exit Strategy Plan A' doesn't look promising. Time to move on to 'Exit Strategy Plan B: Consider the Not So Obvious.'"

This was the part where you acted as if you wanted to be here; as if you knew exactly what you were doing. And then you started to take the deal apart to find the flaw and fix it. I loved the challenge of a struggling deal; I could not bear not to be challenged. The harder it got, the worse it looked, the more I loved it.

Usually, Plan B worked. I discovered that yes, you could learn quite a bit by taking the deal apart and studying it. If you were willing to honestly assess it and took the time it required—if you were patient—you could find the source of the problem. Then, and only then, with ingenious talent, you could rebuild the structure of the investment into a workable, even successful 'makeover.'

I could not wait to apply Plan B to my current situation in the castle. It was time to dig in and begin the adventure. I threw my head back and squared my shoulders. I dared anyone or anything to stand in my way.

Chapter iii

I sat down on the cold stone floor, glad for once that I had an ample backside to provide some cushion and delay the penetration of the inevitable chill. I was ready to implement my favorite strategy and no amount of discomfort would dissuade me.

When an investment went bad (or was in the process of doing so), I always relied on one of my secret weapons, one that no one else saw me use—one that no one else ever thought to use. I called it 'Retracing the Steps,' and it had worked well for me whenever a twist of fate turned an investment sour. I would simply go back to the start of the deal and study its history until I found its inherent weakness.

It was like directing a play. The economic influences were the characters; the deal was the story; the investors were the audience—the critics who rated the performance and decided if I would direct the next play. All I did was direct—which meant I knew exactly what was supposed to happen, and when. If someone or something missed a cue, it was my job to make it work into the performance, as if it were meant to be there. I was a master at my trade.

And I had never had a deal go so badly that I was booed off the stage. No one else had ever had to step in to rescue the deal. And I rescued many. If only someone would write a critical review of my performances as a bank president as they do for actors. My name would be in lights.

I never asked for help. I never told anyone the secret of my success. That would be like Samson telling Delilah he was tired of his hairstyle and needed a haircut. I simply took it upon myself to save the deal because I knew that I was really saving myself. One bad deal was death to a female bank president. One wrong step and the newspaper would pick it up as if it were all that mattered. And I would be ejected from my position like a piece of overdone toast. Dry, charred, and of interest to no one.

Retracing the steps of a deal took time and attention. I had plenty of both to give to my current situation. I would use the same techniques as if I were studying an important financial investment for a client.

Each deal had its own personality, and if I studied it very closely, focusing on it as if nothing else mattered, it would eventually allow me to discover the solution. It felt like a courtship, not that I could speak from any personal experience. But I wooed and won its heart, and then it opened up to me, sharing its innermost secrets.

No one ever studied a deal's history and made it trust them as I did. Oh, sure, they could explain all the adverse influences and create their 'you can't blame me' list of excuses. I took it much further. I continued to take the deal apart and put it back together, until at last, it would reveal its most vulnerable point. Therein would lie the key to turning it around.

Once I knew this, I would develop a strategy to make the deal successful again, or at least respectable. But it was never about blame or excuses. I was never trapped or caught unaware. I watched everything happening at the bank. And everyone who worked for me—especially those in a position to replace me. The motto at the bank became, "If Avery Spencer can't fix it, it can't be fixed." I intended to keep it that way.

So, equipped with my secret weapon, and as the cold from the smooth stone floor seeped into my ample gluteus maximus, I simply decided to apply the same methodology to this situation. It had never failed me in business, and I had nothing to lose here. There had to be a clue that would take me away from here, back to my real world. So I began the looking back to see where the secret key was hidden.

Chapter iv

It had all started on what you might consider a disheartening Saturday with my financial woes. Does it sound strange for a bank president to have personal money problems? Especially a bank president with Master's degrees in both business management and finance? I can offer no explanation. It was my only weakness, and one that I had learned to hide from everyone.

The fact was that I could take care of everyone's finances except my own. And as good as I was at managing everyone else's money, I was that effective at creating my own financial devastation. Whatever I did, I did wholeheartedly.

I had worked long and hard to get to the position of bank president. I was proud of that accomplishment, even if the fact that I was a woman had been the thing that had finally pushed me into the corner office five years ago.

Community complaints that the bank was full of men and the insinuation of discrimination had finally opened that door for me. No, I didn't start the insinuation. But I did use it to my advantage. (Could it have been the column I ran under a pseudonym one month in the local newspaper called *Gender Bias in Small Town America: Does It Still Exist?*

Trust me, I deserved the promotion. I had proven over and over again that I could manage millions of dollars, as long as they didn't belong to me. No one needed to know my terrible secret. I was now middle-aged, well established, and should have been pretty much in a 'coasting' mode. That's the image I projected to the world, and the one I believed in most of the time.

It was incredible when I thought about it. I had come from a blue-collar family, and my parents, neither of whom had ever had the chance to go to college, who had struggled to finance my education, were so proud that I had finally made something of myself. They had sacrificed everything for me. I could never take them into my confidence about my financial problems. Not after all they had done for me. The shame would have been unbearable.

After years of watching me try to climb the banking industry ladder, undated, unmated, and having to explain patiently to family, friends, and neighbors that "No, Avery hasn't met anyone yet," my parents could finally brag about me. I wasn't married, but at least I was a bank president, and that made them feel OK about having a spinster daughter.

Marriage might have been an economic solution to my financial dilemma, but men had never held much interest for me. And it had nothing to do with sexual preferences. I'd just been 'overexposed' to them during my years in this male-dominated profession.

I had learned to succeed in spite of what I considered men's incestuous little networks. I had learned to play by their rules and beat them at their own game, but in an artful way so that I didn't appear overtly competitive. They had so much control over my career fortunes; I didn't desire their influence in my personal life. They were distractions from my primary goal in life, which was proving I didn't need one of them, or anyone for that matter. Besides, most men of my age were boringly set in their ways or grappling with ex-spouses and visiting children. I shuddered at the thought.

The only way I felt secure was if I could make it on my own. And I didn't need any distractions like marriage and a family. Looking after my own aging father was all I could handle since my mother's death two years earlier. I thought of him now, lying in a state of confusion at the local nursing home. I was watching him age with no visible means of financial security. It was such agony. I had vowed that this would never happen to me. But I was only fooling myself.

Whatever sparked it, I was obsessed with an overwhelming need to indulge myself. All I really know is that it never entered my head to live any other way or to pursue any other calling. Nothing but the best of everything and plenty of it. Single, respected, and in control of my life—that was all I ever wanted to accomplish.

In spite of my many successes, I knew that I had not accomplished my one true goal: I was not in control of my financial life; I just looked the part. The one thing in life I desired the most eluded me. Opening the mail today with my defenses down had been a painful reminder.

I had to face my financial future. Deeply in debt despite my very respectable income, and with my father languishing away on state aid in a nursing home, I knew I was not prepared. Nothing terrified me more than not being secure. That's why I always was in control in every single area of my life. Except the one that mattered the most.

Chapter v

The sad thing is that the day had started off as one of those quiet, deliciously warm, perfect autumn Saturdays just before the holiday season. I had gotten out of the bank around one o'clock and headed home with no fundraisers and no social obligations on my calendar for the rest of the weekend. It would be the last such free time for me for many weeks. My best friend, Evelyn, was out of the country, so I had the entire time to myself, which was pretty unusual, and, I thought, a rare treasure.

It was warm enough to drive with the top down on my luxurious silver convertible, and probably one of the last days before the late autumn chill would force me to close the top for the next five months. I just loved the feeling of the air on my face, and the look of pride on the faces of the people I passed as I waved to them over the top of the car. "Well, there goes our bank president," I could just hear them saying. "Doesn't she look smart? And one of our own folks, too."

I thrived on that. I focused on things like how I looked to others—how the sun shone on my copper-red hair. And I didn't give myself much time to go any deeper into my life. As long as I could stick to the surface, I was fine.

The street I lived on was lined with mature silver maple trees. They were in full color, and it felt as though I were moving slowly through an exquisite painting. That's just how my life felt that day—picture perfect.

After parking my stunning little set of wheels in the garage of my upper-class, two-story, four-bedroom, colonial red brick, in-just-the-right-neighborhood suburban home, I turned to gaze admiringly at the car once more as I walked into the house. Such a gorgeous car, and so fitting for a bank president.

The house was immaculate, which meant that Martha had been in today. I inhaled the telltale scent of lemon oil polish that she always used on the furniture, and I knew that after the simple dinner she had prepared for me, which tonight I would eat alone by candlelight, I would eventually enjoy a rose-scented bath surrounded by candles and then slide into bed between soft, clean sheets. Sheer bliss. Perfect.

But right now I had hours of time to savor. It was going to be a marvelous weekend, I decided. I could just relax and do whatever I chose. Feeling that this was a special event that deserved a celebration, I walked through the kitchen, into the temperature-controlled wine room, and pulled out a bottle of my favorite Chardonnay. Ghastly expensive but oh, so divine.

The monogrammed crystal wine glasses, hanging on a wrought-iron rack overhead, chimed softly against one another as I lifted one down.

What a great idea this room had been when I had planned the renovation of my home. Costly, yes, but indispensable for entertaining, which I did often. I removed the cork from the bottle with my stainless steel, single-action bottle opener and poured a glass of the liquid gold for myself. Raising it to the ceiling to propose a toast to a great weekend, I saluted the air, then put the bottle in a sterling silver bucket of ice and took it with me as I headed outdoors to enjoy the warm fall sunshine before the evening chill set in.

Stepping outside through the French doors just off the breakfast nook, I surveyed my expansive backyard, the inviting pool, and stately gardens. I inhaled the fresh air and drank in the lovely view along with my wine. What a wonderful life I had!

My gardens were as immaculate as my home, thanks mostly to Peter, my caretaker. I loved gardening, and had created garden beds that mysteriously expanded each year along with the number of garden magazines I subscribed to. "Garden of the Year" awards were now quite commonplace for my home, and each framed certificate was mounted modestly in the hallway to the guest bathroom. No one could miss them, but no one could accuse me of being arrogant about them, either.

I could not possibly maintain the extensive gardens on my own any longer. Peter was a gift from heaven, absolutely meticulous about meeting my increasingly demanding requirements, as long as I paid his increasingly large bills. He also tended the pool. Just thinking of him with his shirt off made me wish I were younger.

I smiled to myself while I made a mental note to remind him that next week we should begin the fall cleanup and prepare to close the pool. Never one to be still for long, I drained my glass of wine, officially ending my brief reverie, and headed back into the house, wine bucket and empty wine glass in hand.

Chapter vi

Feeling rather satisfied with myself, I set my wine glass and ice bucket on the granite breakfast bar that framed the renovated kitchen work area. Walking upstairs to my wonderful sage-green master bedroom, trimmed with white crown and floor molding, I could not help but be happy here. My queen-sized, walnut, Victorian canopy bed was the focal point of the room. Martha had pulled back the garden tapestry duvet bedcover. The crisp, ironed white Egyptian cotton monogrammed pillowcases and sheets looked almost too tempting to resist.

But I had hours before bedtime. I walked past the bed into my substantial closet, which my mother had laughingly called the 'guest room.' I missed her since her death and had to smile at the memory. She had been right, as usual. It was large enough to be a guest room. Complete with dressing area and a triple full-length, beveled-glass mirror, it was specifically organized and maintained to my painstaking requirements.

Changing from my designer navy pantsuit into my favorite jeans, I thought momentarily about how much I spent on my attire. My clothing was expensive but, I argued often to myself, so necessary and appropriate for my position. In the early days of being the bank's president, my friend Evelyn and I used to shriek with horrified delight at spending so much money for clothing worthy of my position. We shopped at only the finest boutiques, sometimes traveling to New York City to make certain we lived on the cutting edge of fashion. Now, however, my closets were full of fine clothes, all clean and ready to wear at a moment's notice. All I ever had to worry about was paying for them.

It would never do to appear soft and feminine at the bank as I negotiated serious financial transactions. No one would take me seriously if I looked too 'cute.' No, I would rather err on the side of looking elegantly authoritative, even severe. Money was a serious matter, and I wanted to be sure I looked the part of a responsible, mature, confident bank president.

Always careful with my appearance, I hated ever wearing the same outfit more than once. Martha helped me keep track, and Evelyn and I added scarves and pins to make the outfit look different so that no one could tell if I did occasionally repeat an outfit. Even at home, if the neighbors in my subdivision saw me outdoors or if someone came to the door, I felt compelled to look the part of a successful businesswoman.

In contrast to my extensive business wardrobe, my at-home attire was rather boring, but stylish. After stepping into my jeans, I put on one of my white, monogrammed, oxford cloth button-down shirts expertly pressed by Martha, buttoning all but the top two buttons, and leaving it untucked. Selecting a clean pair of tennis shoes from the closet, I walked over to the mirror to study my appearance. I knew I was no beauty—my form was bottom heavy, but I was fit for my age. And my trainer, Margot, kept me looking that way.

My copper-red hair was my 'crowning glory,' as my father called it, and I shook it loose from the upswept look I always wore for the bank. Only at home did I wear my hair down, which Evelyn was careful to point out to me was not quite the same as 'letting your hair down,' which she claimed I did not do very well.

It took special chemicals to achieve the color, but as it fell casually over my shoulders, I relaxed and smiled at the lovely face in the mirror. I slipped on my tennis shoes. No socks. My ankles looked thinner without them.

Not bad, Avery Victoria Spencer, I thought. Not bad at all for the little girl whose only claims to fame in school had been excellent grades, a flair for numbers, and running a tip-top audio-visual department in both middle school and high school. (With a nickname like 'A.V.' and a chunky figure, it was hard to think of joining the cheerleading squad.) No one used a nickname with me anymore. And, while there wasn't any audio-visual equipment I couldn't run, I kept my mouth shut at the bank and let others handle the job. That skill had never appeared on any of my resumes.

I headed back down to the kitchen, stopping to put my favorite classical baroque CD on the sound system that ran throughout the house. In a matter of seconds, the symphony wooed me into an even more tranquil state. Blissfully I filled my wine glass a second time and sat down to open the day's mail that Martha had stacked neatly on the breakfast bar before she left.

It was the worst thing I could have chosen to do on such a golden day.

Chapter vii

I hated the mail. It never brought me much of anything now except shopping catalogs and bills. Horrid bills: first and second mortgage payments (it had cost a fortune to renovate the house), car payment, utility bills, whopping credit card bills with late payment interest charges, invoices from Martha's cleaning service, and Peter's landscaping service. I paid Margot in cash each week.

Once a quarter, I would get my retirement fund statement, and today just happened to be that day. Picking up my favorite pearl-handled letter opener that I had purchased on my trip to Italy with Evelyn last year, my anxiety escalated as it did every time I confronted my financial future. It was the only thing in my life that wasn't perfect—the one aspect that taunted me in quiet moments like this one.

I always tried to keep my mood light when I looked at the picture my retirement fund statement painted for me. But invariably, I could feel the familiar spiraling descent to despair begin. Today would be no exception. Not even a six-figure salary could feed the financial monster I had created. Yes, I had some money put away, but not as much as I could have, and certainly not enough to support me in the manner to which I had become accustomed. I had a degree in knowing what my failure to plan now would mean for my future. I took a large gulp of wine and then another.

My quarterly retirement fund statements hit me like a financial obituary. I could see it now: "Here lies the financial well-being of Avery Victoria Spencer. Over the course of her lifetime, she succeeded in misusing the money she had made as president of our bank and spent herself into ruin. She resides now at the city's low-income housing project, Desperate Arms Apartments, alone and miserable, not getting any sympathy from the other residents who live there because life never gave them the breaks it gave her."

I tried to reassure myself. This home was a sound financial investment. But it was the early release of my inheritance money that my parents had painstakingly saved over the years that had provided the modest down payment. The mortgage payments still took my breath away each month, especially because I had such significant credit card debt.

It was shocking to be earning as much as I did and still feel like I was living 'paycheck to paycheck,' just as I always had. So while no one would think that a bank president could have such financial woes, I knew it, subconsciously, every waking minute.

I just kept myself busy enough to not think about it. Except for this weekend.

There was never enough money. I danced between financial obligations like a whirling dervish. If I could just dance fast enough, I figured my creditors couldn't catch me. But dancing fast just means you are spinning out of control, and when you fall to the ground and the world stops spinning, nothing has changed. I was trapped, imprisoned by my financial woes.

Now I remembered why being busy was so necessary. And why I never stopped 'the dance.' If I ever sat down to catch my breath, I would know. If I waited for the world to stop spinning, I would be able to see the prison bars, feel the weight of my burden, and know I was not free.

I reached for my glass of wine. Without realizing it, I had already finished the second glass. Two was always my limit. Such discipline! But today, two was not enough. To hell with discipline—the demons in my mind were going to have a heyday if I didn't do something quickly. I uncorked the now half-empty bottle and refilled my glass, hoping that a third one would relax my anxious feelings and drug my demons.

.

Chapter viii

And so, the bliss of a weekend alone evaporated like the mist on California's Highway 1 that shrouds travelers' views of the breathtaking but treacherous precipice upon which they travel. I now had to face the financial precipice on which I lived.

On the surface, I was living well, the way a bank president should. But it tortured me constantly, because I, of all people, knew better. I was so damned smart about money… my Master's degrees and my *cum laude* status at graduation had proven that. I had all the knowledge and facts, and I could run a successful financial operation.

But I could not manage my own financial life. I had never been able to. Each monetary step up on the financial ladder seemed like the magic number that would enable me to live within my means. The next rung was always the solid gold one, I told myself. But it was an illusion. Today, when my means were larger than I had ever dreamed, I still could not live within them. And I knew it was just getting worse. The demons were dancing.

Perhaps the hardest reality was that the small city in which I lived respected me and extolled me as an example of success. I constantly sought solace in that. I was a featured speaker for many civic causes. I wrote a monthly financial column in the Business Gazette, advising people on sound investment strategies.

I knew that in the eyes of so many people, women especially, I epitomized the meaning of the word 'success.' I worked hard to make sure that image did not disappoint them. But inside, on the rare occasion that I stopped to think about it, I felt like a sham, and it scared me. So I made it a point not to stop and not to think. 'Dance, Avery, dance!' I tried to tell myself as I sat staring at the 'Past Due' notices in front of me. But I was too tired.

Sighing heavily, I pushed myself away from the counter, leaving the stack of mail strewn over the marble surface. Normally, I would have called Evelyn at this point, and she would have helped me laugh my way back into nonchalance. But Evelyn was on sabbatical from the University, touring Europe with a group of other professors. Relying on my own scant resources for dealing with emotional challenges, I brilliantly decided to finish my third glass of wine and just lie down for a few minutes to rest before I faced reality. Who says a few glasses of wine and a nap can't solve problems?

Chapter ix

I headed to the beautiful sunroom just off the kitchen that also overlooked the pool and gardens in the back of the house. It was a relaxed setting, perfect for all kinds of casual activities, including napping. The early evening sun was just setting and had I not been so despondent, I would have reveled in its glory.

Decorated in soft yellows and greens with lavender and rose accents, this room and all the others in my home had been the artistic accomplishment of George, my decorator, who had listened carefully to the environment I wanted to live in. Outdoor gardens were not enough. I wanted to bring them indoors and he had created wonderful rooms of soft color pallets, each room like entering a different garden. I loved this room most of all and often entertained here, especially on warm summer evenings.

Sometimes it was just Evelyn and me. She would kick one of her long legs over the arm of the wicker rocker and use the other leg to rock it back and forth. Evelyn had a 'devil-may-care' attitude about money that seemed to work for her. No matter how dismal things might look financially, she'd just keep spending, and the money she needed would show up somehow—in bucketfuls. I was deeply jealous of her good fortune. Emulating her attitude for years, I never realized that one can't pretend to have a casual attitude about money and get the same results as someone else who really does. I just went deeper into debt.

Other times, I would have evening dinners or drinks and hors d'oeuvres (prepared by Martha, of course), and neighbors, bank personnel, or civic leaders would be invited. Twice each year, I had an open house. In the summer it was an evening party with chamber music in the backyard, and at holiday time there was a chamber orchestra indoors. I would amaze guests with the beautiful award-winning gardens in the summer and impress them with the festive decorating each winter. Every event would be a fundraiser for a favorite charity. Pictures of the locally famous and the amount of their contributions were published in the city newspaper each year. And I had to be at the top of the list, didn't I?

As I collapsed miserably on the sofa, trying to soothe my troubled mind, I could not summon the repertoire of excuses and rationalizations that normally consoled me. It was as if I had crossed an invisible threshold this time, and I knew the old arguments just wouldn't hold up anymore. They were like worn-out garments. Washed once too often and disintegrated, I had no more ready-to-wear excuses hanging in the closet of my mind. I was shamefully unprepared.

I was glad no one else knew, but at the same time, feeling sorry for myself, I ached for someone to confide in... someone who could help me out of this awful mess. I carried this burden alone just like everything else. My parents had never encouraged me to confide in them—in fact, I had always felt as if I needed to impress them or at least spare them from the truth. By now, this façade was just a habit I couldn't break. Besides, before my mother was gone, she would just have patted my hand and said, "Well, honey, I tried to warn you..." And my father was not reachable on this level. Funny thing... neither was I.

My determination had always gotten me through the tough times in my life, but this felt too big even for my immense coping capability. I needed to talk to someone. I needed to find an answer before it was too late. I needed help badly, and didn't know where to turn. I already knew everything there was to know about money and money management. This was beyond my own power to change.

"Help me," I said softly into the sunlit air. "Help me." The wine and music washed over me. I simply fell asleep with these thoughts on my mind.

My soul must have interpreted my words as a prayer, and this castle must have something to do with the answer. I had retraced my steps—now I could move on. Yes, Plan B had to work.

Chapter x

And so, sitting here in the castle and using my Plan B strategy, I had the first clue to the reason that I was here in this dank, dark room with no discernable way back to my life. I was on a journey to learn the answer to my questions about money. Or something like that. My cry for help must have been heard. I was intrigued.

Intrigued, yes, but trapped. The light from the torches seemed to prove that there was no means of escape. Curious now that I sensed a reason for being here and determined to be a quick learner, I decided to revisit the room and explore it in greater detail. There had to be something here that I had missed on my first inspection. Besides, my backside was now numb; the cold had crept through my skin and into my sitting bones. I jumped up, rubbed my gluts to get some blood circulating, and began sleuthing the room. It seemed different somehow.

My hunch turned out to be correct. As I studied the room more intently, I noticed a strange stone wall formation that I had not seen before. I walked toward it, eager to discover what it was. As I got closer, I instinctively sensed that this was a way toward somewhere—I hoped somewhere that would reveal more about why I was here.

I peered around the corner of the wall and saw by the light of the torches lining its curve what appeared to be a spiral stone staircase leading down, deeper into the castle. Since nothing led anywhere else, it seemed obvious I should move in that direction. If I was going to proceed at all. And of course I was. I hadn't gotten to be the president of a bank by being a sissy, and now was no time to start. I yearned to get to the bottom of my financial woes and if going to the bottom of this staircase would help, I was only too glad to continue. The sooner, the better.

As I entered the landing at the top of the staircase, an encouraging sight caught my attention—a single white pillar candle was sitting on the balustrade, its flame seeming to dance with a sense of delight, as if begging to accompany me on the journey.

It was not just any candle, but a beautifully molded one like from those centuries past when candles were considered valuable and magical. In earlier times people believed that these candles could bring blessing and healing. They would shape them even in shapes of body parts that needed to be made whole. But more often they were molded, as this one appeared to be, with a favorite symbol.

As I picked up this wonderful, brave light and turned it in my hands, I noticed the figure of a swan with wings spread and head tucked gently that molded into opposite sides of the candle. The body of the swan formed a winged shape, like the letter 'S', the first letter of my last name.

I smiled at what I saw, not only because of the shape of the letter, but also because I loved swans. Their beauty and grace, their transformation process. The story of the Ugly Duckling had filled an ache in my heart as a child, because I felt so much like one myself. I had always hoped to one day be a beautiful swan. That story, long forgotten, came back to me now as I held the candle in my hands.

It was a heavy, sturdy pillar, one that would last for quite a while. Long enough, I hoped, to get me through this exploration. And it was such a happy thing in this dismal place, the flame leaping for joy as if excited to see me. Strange, I thought, but encouraging.

And so, with a warm heart and freezing body, I welcomed the light of the candle for the darkness of the journey that might lie ahead. What a loving gesture for one who had always been spooked by the darkness. I felt strangely cared for. Not that I needed it, you understand, but nevertheless, I was glad for it. Yes, a candle in this strange place was a good sign.

My shadow loomed ominously next to me, shining larger than life on the wall as I proceeded cautiously downward, around and around, stepping carefully onto each pie-shaped stone step, going deeper into the castle. The staircase was narrow; I could not stretch my arms out in both directions. I used my left hand for support against the cold, rough-hewn, and uneven stone wall, which was heavily mortared to hold the stones in place. Another sign of antiquity.

With the other hand, I held the candle out in front of me so that I could see my way. The only sounds came from my squeaking tennis shoes on each stone step. And my breathing.

The lighted torches I had seen at the top of the staircase continued downward but became fewer in number and farther apart. Finally, only the light from my candle guided me to the next step.

I felt a little bit like mystery sleuth Nancy Drew, whose stories had left me delightfully terrified in the middle of the night as a young girl. Unable to sleep once I started reading, I would finish the book, always trying, but rarely beating Nancy at solving the mystery. Then I would lie wide awake the rest of the night until early daylight reassured me that the sinister characters from the story were not hiding behind my door or under my bed. Only then would I sleep. Insatiable, I would beg my mother for the next volume to add to my collection. I had them all and considered them among my 'in case of a fire, grab these first' possessions.

In that context, this mysterious journey suited me just fine, as long as I sensed there was nothing dangerous going on. My candle seemed so happy that it was hard to believe there was anything ahead that I should fear. Just as I had found the imaginary terror of the unknown fascinating back in childhood, it lured me now. Besides, I was a mature adult, in the prime of her life. I'd survived enough of the hard parts of growing up. I wasn't going to play scared now.

Chapter xi

As the staircase wound almost dizzily downward, the air seemed to become colder, and I shivered even more, which I told myself was from the chill, not nervousness. My toes turned stiff and cold in my woefully inadequate tennis shoes. In spite of my bravado, in spite of the reassurance of the candle, I knew nothing about where I was or where this journey would lead. Still, I simply refused to be afraid. If I admitted I was, I would have become paralyzed.

I just kept taking each step downward. Something was drawing me forward on this quest, perhaps many things. Curiosity, for one. Mine was insatiable. But also the belief that there was a reason I was here and not just that I had had a little too much to drink when I lay down for a nap. The candle with its dancing flame and swan symbol for example, intertwined with my love of mystery and old castles. For many reasons, I continued.

I did have a terribly curious nature and an acute sense of intuitiveness—or, as my mother had called it, my 'doom radar.' It was beyond pessimism, which was just a negative perspective of things. My own personal radar was attuned to sensing there was something wrong, if indeed there was, before it revealed itself. It had probably saved me from more bad dates than the fact that there weren't many compelling reasons for a man to want to get to know me better unless he had a terrible need to torture himself.

No, my radar was not pessimism, but it was another one of those gifts that I hid from others because it made me feel different. I even tried to hide it from myself, until I understood its power to inform me on a sensory level. It had more than once sent me on a fascinating investigation when I sensed something was wrong at the bank but couldn't put my finger on it.

Like the time we had been ready to sign on as the primary lender in a new mall across town. It was an area of the community that was growing and showed promise. A mall would be just the thing to encourage more residential and commercial development. It made perfect sense.

But from the onset, my 'doom radar' was on high alert. Everyone at the bank was pushing for the deal to close, anxiously ignoring my hesitation, which they had learned to value and loathe all at the same time. Putting our name on the sign meant significant publicity... and better us than any of our competitors, right? Even my key advisors kept minimizing my instincts and trying to bring the project in.

I had learned to trust this sensitivity. To ignore it was to fail. I could not shake the sense that something was not right. Moving forward with the utmost care and secrecy, I decided to become my own private detective in order to prove whether my instincts were correct or not. And of course they were, but it was never good enough for a bank president to say no to the biggest project in the city's history just because she had a bad feeling to it. No, I had to have compelling proof. Or the Board of Directors could override me—the kiss of death to my future.

So I studied and researched what was behind this 'too good to be true' project. While everything looked amazing on paper, my detective work paid off. Contacts with old business associates and trusted advisors... a drink or two with colleagues of colleagues of colleagues, and so on.

Quietly and quickly, and oh so subtly, without anyone even knowing what they were telling me, I picked up that this group's latest project was not only behind schedule, but about 37 percent over budget. Already. Which I learned was hidden by some untraceable, exaggerated fancy pencil work to make the project look good to prospective investors.

But behind the spreadsheet mask, there was another deal that had not worked and the purpose of this 'too good to be true' project was to create a cash cover-up for the appetite of the starving monster camouflaged in dollars and cents—the one that ate cash like kids eat candy on Halloween. Only it had to be fed every day, and it just got hungrier. One deal had to feed the last one.

The developer desperately needed this transaction to close to support the cash losses on others, which were supporting the ones before that. And while the concept of a mall was good and the location was superb, the foundation of the project was built out of wobbling dominoes. All it would take was a push and the whole empire would collapse.

Once I presented my findings to the Board, we unanimously decided to turn down the deal. We pushed the first domino over. The local media was shocked by what it considered the biggest public mistake of my financial reign.

But not for long. The group's foundation collapsed as one financial domino hit the next one with such blinding speed that in only a matter of weeks the whole empire crashed. It wasn't long until the company was only a memory with a number of larger banks mourning their losses. A loss of this magnitude would have put our own vibrant financial institution into cardiac arrest.

Curiosity might have killed the cat, but it kept me alive. I had learned to love my curiosity and to pay attention to my 'doom radar.' Cats may have nine lives, but this female bank president had only one.

On this inspiring memory and sensing no vibration on my 'doom radar' frequency, I reached the bottom of the staircase, which revealed a hallway lit only by a single torch at its entrance. Otherwise, it looked dark and uninviting—darkness reaching into eternity. But it was clearly the only option to turning around and heading back up the staircase, which I knew led nowhere else.

I was cold, tired, and now disappointed. All this way, and I had arrived exactly nowhere. Another dead end. I expected more cooperation if this journey was to help me to discover the secret of my financial agony. No, I didn't need a red carpet welcome and full illumination with neon signs flashing at every turn, but surely I deserved some clarity.

I frowned and sat down on the last step for a moment to get my bearings and to pout a bit. I looked at my candle, as if it might have some idea of what to do next. But it only danced brightly as always. After a few moments of stillness, the cold sank deeper into my bones. I couldn't just sit here, I realized. There was a way to go, even though where it would take me wasn't clear from where I sat.

Finally my bank president's mind kicked into gear again. There was nothing wrong with taking the next step to see how it felt and where it led. I wasn't making an irrevocable decision. Was I? I could turn back at any time. Couldn't I? As long as I hadn't signed a contract. Or had I?

I decided to go just a short way down the hall, and if nothing revealed itself, I'd decide what to do then. I picked up my candle and proceeded past the light of the torch. The hallway got darker and darker. I strained my eyes for some sort of encouragement. And finally, in the black ink darkness, I was rewarded by seeing what appeared to be a thin golden beam of light shining in the distance. It could have been an illusion, but I felt encouraged and walked eagerly, but cautiously, toward it.

Chapter xii

The hallway ended abruptly. The light from my candle revealed what looked like a door in front of me. The light I had seen in the distance was coming from under this door.

There was no way to go forward without entering this room. Fine with me. The fewer the options, the easier the decision. Holding my candle in my left hand, I moved the light up and down, trying to find a latch to open the door. As I groped with my right hand, I felt the heavy planks of wood that made up the door, worn smooth with age, and held together by wrought iron bands.

At last I was rewarded for my efforts. I found the latch and pushed down on it to enter the room. But the door did not budge. I was certain that I was holding the latch in the open position. I put my weight against it, but the door simply did not respond. Obviously, it had not been opened in a very, very long time.

Now, I'm not a weakling. I might be a woman, but I've taken care of myself, thank you very much. I have lifted some decent weights over the years. As I mentioned earlier, my personal trainer, Margot, has been a faithful and devoted instructor. I plan to age well, and she sees to it that I do the work I need to remain strong.

This door, however, was going to be another challenge. Fine. I set the candle down, grabbed, pushed, and yanked at the door with both hands. But my 'I shall overcome this' attitude wasn't working. The door was heavy and stubborn. It was as if it were nailed shut from the inside. Even in my fine physical condition, I was no match for the task at hand.

The door seemed to mock my efforts as I pushed with all my strength. Exhausted, and rather put out, I finally gave up and sat down on the icy floor. I picked up my faithful candle and contemplated my next move.

"This is all your fault," I said to the candle. (Did the flame dim at my reprimand, or was I only imagining it?) That was a frightening thought. The last thing I needed was an unhappy candle that might decide to extinguish itself because of my lousy attitude.

"Sorry," I said. It brightened.

As I sat there in the cold quiet, I suddenly heard the latch unhook, and watched in disbelief as the door began to open into the room. I gasped... I honestly didn't know whether to be terrified or relieved. Or to feel a little bit sheepish at my

ridiculous attempts to force the door open with my brute
strength. Perhaps knocking would have been a good idea.

The opening door moved slowly, taking its time. But little
by little, it gave in, its hinges moaning and groaning with each
inch of progress, just like in a horror movie. I was so relieved
that I grabbed my candle and, as soon as I could clear enough
space, squeezed past the opening door and into the room. The
door immediately snapped shut behind me.

Once inside, I looked around to see who had opened the
door. But no one appeared to be there. As I studied this room,
the first thing I noticed from my vantage point near the door
was that the large room appeared to be empty except for two
stone pillars at equal distance from the walls in the center of the
room, and a marvelously bright fire in a massive stone hearth on
the far wall.

Warmth and light. The fire provided the only light in the
room and must have been what drew me from far down the
hallway. But the rest of the room remained dark since the light
of the fire could not reach its full width and breadth. I decided
I would explore later, after savoring the warmth of the fire.

As I headed eagerly closer to the fire, the heat began to
move into my body. I had not realized just how cold I was until
my body trembled from the shock of the heat meeting the
surface of my skin. It was almost painful. I had to back away

from the fire at first, and then move very slowly toward it in order to accept its healing warmth. I placed my candle gently on the wooden mantle above the hearth where it seemed to blaze even more brightly than before. With both hands free, I could rub them together until the heat loosened their frozen joints and I could flex them easily.

It took some time for me to feel completely warm, and I stood basking in front of the fire until my shivering stopped. I had never known the absolute joy of returning to warmth from the deep freeze of a cold castle. Even my bones celebrated.

The blazing fire had captured my full attention at first, but now curiosity returned to this puzzling journey. Feeling more like myself, I reached for the candle, thinking to explore my surroundings a bit more. At least this room had an exit. I glanced over at the door to make certain it was still there. It was.

With candle in hand once again, I stepped away from the fireplace and noticed in so doing that the wooden hearth was elegantly carved in the center with the same queenly swan that was molded into both sides of my candle. I was encouraged, but only for a moment.

Studying the ornate carving in the middle of the mantle, I suddenly realized that I was staring at my own initials scripted beautifully into the wood. Wait a minute. It looked like a medieval coat of arms: the S was the shape of the swan. The A and V on either side of the swan could not be mistaken. Perhaps I should have been pleased, or at least reassured, but this time the unmistakable personalization troubled me. With the candle, I assumed that the S was merely a reassuring coincidence. Now it felt more like ownership.

Did the coat of arms signify that I owned the castle? And if this were my own castle, why was it so foreboding, unwelcoming, and mysterious? I frowned. The candle danced wildly as if saying, "Yes, yes, yes! This is your castle!" It at least seemed to be overjoyed at my discovery. I had to smile in spite of myself. But I still was not sure that I was pleased with the revelation.

At least I was warm. I decided to search the room for clues to the next step on this puzzling journey. Whether I liked it or not, I knew for certain now that I was supposed to be here. How I felt about that was clearly beside the point.

Walking away from the fire and into the darkness around the walls of the chamber, I suddenly struck something on the floor. As I moved my candle to identify the object, I shrieked in horror when I saw that I had tripped over a pair of bare, bony feet. As the light of my now-shaking candle moved almost in spite of itself, (and absolutely against my better judgment), it cast its glow on what looked to be the skeletal remains of an old, old man in dusty rags, bound in irons to the stone wall. My castle had a prisoner?

Four heavy chains were secured to the wall. As my eyes followed the strong links downward, I saw that two of the chains attached to hinged iron bands secured with locks on each of his two wrists. The other two were secured to his ankles. Clearly medieval, clearly sturdy. Without a doubt, this old man had been here a very, very long time.

I was glad that I could not see the poor wretch's face, as his head had fallen on his chest. His gray, disheveled beard hid the lower part of his face, and his long, thin hair hung forward, shrouding the rest of his face from view. There was no telling whether he was alive or dead.

Suddenly, I had had enough. I was tired of being spooked at every turn, given a bit of hope, another clue, and then more bad news. I was physically exhausted from the cold and now mentally undone by the sight before me. I was suddenly scared, trembling with fear. Dead man or alive, I wasn't about to try to find out which. It was time to drop the cavalier bank president image. There was no one to impress here. I was terrified. Without stopping to question further, I stepped cautiously over the feet and headed toward the door I had come in.

Chapter xiii

"You will find that there is no exit from this room, my friend," I heard a voice say quietly and firmly but with a great gasping effort. I froze dead in my tracks. This was far beyond any fear I had faced in my lifetime. This felt real. Sheer dread iced my being. For a moment, I could not move. I could not breathe. I was certain my heart had stopped beating. I will never know what brought me back into the scene that was unfolding. But suddenly I was gasping for breath and my heart was beating wildly as if racing to catch up.

Who had spoken? I turned in shock to the only other human being in the room to see if he had uttered the words that still reverberated in echoes around me. Surely not this skeletal carcass. But who else?

"W-who said that?" I squeaked. I cleared my throat for a better delivery. "Who said that?" I tried a more authoritative tone.

"I did," the voice replied, gasping. Yes, it was definitely coming from the old man. He must be alive, then. But barely. I hadn't an ounce of medical background, but even I could tell the man spoke with a great effort, his breathing labored.

He did not look up at me as he spoke. Perhaps that would require too much effort. Inching a little closer to him, I held my candle up and was amazed to see the almost imperceptible rise and fall of his bony chest.

How is it possible that he is alive? I wondered. Still, I was relieved that he was chained. It meant that he posed no physical threat to me.

"Who are you?" I asked again, this time more demanding. Fear always made me angry. Part of me hoped he would not respond—the part that didn't want to take this journey any further. The other, braver, and hopelessly more curious part of me, wanted to solve this mystery, and willed him to stay alive just a little longer. But still, he had frightened me. He owed me an explanation as long as there was breath in his body.

I knew he was there for a reason... a reason I needed to know. This was my castle. I had a vague sense that something inside of me was creating what was transpiring here. He just might be the clue I needed to get the message and leave this awful place. If only he would speak to me again.

My need to know outweighed my fear of knowing—at least for the moment. Continuing to approach him cautiously, I held my candle out in front of me like a protective shield, while scolding myself for being frightened by a dying old man. Bound in chains to boot.

My anger subsided as I knelt beside him on the dusty, cold floor, carefully trying to stay outside of his limited range of motion. Through the dark, worn rags that barely covered him, I could see the gaunt frame of the old man. He looked like a skeleton draped with loose skin that could not resist the sinking pull of gravity wherever there was no bone to support it.

The old scars and bloody marks on his wrists and ankles from the iron shackles made it apparent that he had made some futile attempts to escape. He didn't look like anyone to be afraid of, but in this strange place, I wasn't taking any chances.

"Who are you?" I asked again, this time pleading for a response.

He seemed to ignore my words. Instead he choked out, "Avery Victoria Spencer, you've come at last!" His slowly delivered words were punctuated by labored breathing and obvious emotion.

He knew me? He was expecting me? Why was I so surprised?

"I... I... I'm sorry, sir," I stammered. "I don't believe we have met before. Could you be thinking of someone else?" Stupid question, he's thinking. He knew my name.

He smiled sadly and spoke again, each word still sounding like his last. "Oh, dear Avery," he almost wept as he spoke, "I have been trapped here for many, many years, waiting patiently for you to come. I had given up all hope. I know that you don't recognize me, but I know you so well. Please come closer and prop me up a little so I can get a good look at you and so I do not have to speak with such effort."

Well, what could it hurt? He sounded so genuine, and I guess I was always a sucker for frail old skeletons. Except that I would have to get close enough to touch him. That frightened me. Why did I suddenly feel like Little Red Riding Hood meeting the Big Bad Wolf?

"OK," I agreed, "but only if you promise to tell me who you are and how I can get out of this place." That was my style, you see, always playing tough and negotiating a way out.

He nodded his drooped head slightly in the affirmative. After setting my candle down, I stood facing him and placed my left hand under his right arm and then reached across his body to his left arm. Lifting gently, to be sure not to leave any of his loosely frail body parts behind, I helped him sit up. I could feel the skin sliding across his bones, which hung loosely in their joints. After settling him into a sort of upright posture, I sat down cross-legged at his side, ignoring the dust. I brought the candle in closer, and his aged, sad face suddenly seemed to be framed in a golden light.

Chapter xiv

His breathing improved immediately, as did mine. I was surprised to find that my own had become labored, as if I had been trying to help him breathe.

"Tell me why you have finally come," he inquired.

It was flattering, you know, to think that I had kept a guy waiting for me. And that he had actually waited. For a lifetime it appeared.

"I am not certain how I have come to be here," I told him honestly. "But I have been burdened with great despair over my personal finances today and woke up in this place. Perhaps you can help me."

This seemed to take a while to register with him. Either that or it took him that long to get enough strength to answer. "Oh, yes," he finally responded. "Now that you are here, we can help each other."

The strange response surprised me. "I'm not sure how I can help you, sir," I replied, "but I am hoping you can help me. Do you know why I am here?" I asked. "Or can you at least tell me where to go from here?"

"A bit self-centered, aren't we?" he replied with sudden disdain. "I'm the one who has been stuck here, in chains, waiting for you to free me, and all you can think of is how you can get out of here? What about me?" The old man shocked me with the intensity of his response. I was more than just a little bit offended. I turned to face him.

"Me, free *you*?" I asked. "I don't even know you!"

"Oh, yes you do," he snapped back. "And only you can rescue me. Surely you know that."

"How can I help *you*?" I asked. "Who are you?"

We were both showing signs of frustration. Which left me totally unprepared for what happened next. Taking both of my hands in an unbreakable grip, this seemingly weak and dying old man turned to look at me fully, his face bright with intense emotion.

"Look at me and tell me you don't know who I am!" he cried in utter anguish. "How is it possible that you do not recognize me? Are you really so blind that you do not recognize your own Spirit of Financial Woes! Take a good look, because you have made me what I am!"

This repulsive declaration echoed around the room, ricocheting and falling around me, assaulting my ears, and driving daggers into my consciousness until my own deafening screams took over.

"No, no, no! You are nothing to me! How dare you try to blame me for your own miserable existence!" I raged as I tried to free my hands from his. I needed them to cover my ears so I could not hear his words. I needed them so I could choke the life out of him. I needed them so I could leave. Anything to keep this revelation from penetrating my awareness.

But he would not let go of me. And even as I struggled, I knew it was too late. I would not forget his words; I knew somewhere deep inside they were true, and I hated him for it—for shocking me into this reality. But it was useless to fight him. At last, I ceased struggling and sat quietly, refusing to accept his message. Everything became still.

Chapter xv

The struggle had cost him dearly. "Promise me you will not leave until I have spoken my piece with you," the old man begged with a weakening voice, now gasping, but full of compassion for me. "If you try to run away, you will find that there is no escape. You may spend the rest of your life longing to know and never understanding, or you can stop and listen now. We do not have much time."

Was he right? Had I come in at the end of a relationship I never knew I had? If he was my Spirit of Financial Woes, I was in trouble. He was the epitome of deprivation, the essence of poverty, the symbol of captivity. And he was on this deathbed, just as my own finances were at a critical stage. I could almost smell the formaldehyde waiting for him, and the faint, familiar odor of funeral home flowers seemed to fill the room. I tried to swallow, but I choked on my fear.

At the same time, as my senses returned, it did cross my mind that if he was right, I should be grateful he was still alive. He could have simply passed out of my life a long time ago. But he had waited patiently. Perhaps I was lucky to have even a few moments with him; perhaps I should be grateful.

"Very well," I responded, subdued. "I will listen to what you have to say."

He released my hands, and I sat back wearily on the floor near him. Too weak to hold his head up any longer, he rested it against the wall and turned his head to face me. I only had to look into his eyes to know that all he was telling me was true. I could not look away.

"My dear Avery, I know this comes as a surprise to you, but I am indeed a physical manifestation of the burden of financial woes that you have been carrying these many years," he began.

"I represent in physical form what you have believed about money. I am the vision you asked for when you lay down today, full of despair. You finally asked for help. And now you should not be so shocked to see me as I am. I have not prospered; neither have you. The irons I wear are the debts, fears, and negative thoughts you have accumulated over the years. It is not pleasant, but it is true."

I had never thought of what my burden might look like in the physical form. But even if I had, it never occurred to me that it would be so awful. I swallowed to fight back the disagreeable and unfamiliar tightness in my throat. What was this? Had he moved me to tears? I would not cry; I never cried.

He went on. "I count my blessings. It is warm enough here, and the room is dry. For this, I thank you. But now you can see in me the poverty and negativity that have been the focus of your attention throughout your life. They have found expression here, in me."

He continued. "You and I aspired to great prosperity and abundance when we were younger. I thought that we would have a fine relationship. You were so talented, so creative, so alive with possibility.

"Sadly, however, it became clear as time passed that you had no real intention of learning the secrets of achieving either true success or prosperity. You were too afraid. You focused your attention, not on that which would express your great and unique contribution to the world—which is the only way to true prosperity—but on how to earn enough money to feel secure and look prosperous to the outside world. In so doing, you gained neither.

"You accomplished much, but as you focused on what you feared, you actually created more fear. You thought by giving the fear attention you could overcome it. But aside from the mere appearance of prosperity, you have never found what you have so earnestly and diligently sought. This has led to the burden you now carry—the illusion of abundance where there is none. This is a false life and a dishonorable way to live."

"Now just a minute," I declared. "There's no need to get mean. I am not a false and dishonorable person, and I resent that insinuation."

"Oh, my dear, dear Avery," groaned my Spirit of Financial Woes, "you suffer from the deepest form of falseness and dishonesty... so much so that you do not recognize it anymore. I have watched you spend your way through thousands of dollars, all to create an illusion of financial security. Even your choice of profession serves this illusion. No one questions the financial position of a bank president, do they? Of course not!

"Yes, you have masked your issue well from others, but never from yourself, and certainly not from me who has suffered the most from your useless quest. The more false your life has become, the more debt you have accumulated, and the farther you have drifted from your own sense of yourself.

"And you have suffered, my dear friend. Maybe not so everyone could see it, but I could. I am your suffering self, Avery Victoria. I have lived your financial reality every waking minute, though you have expended great effort to ignore me. You have imprisoned me here and have never given me a thought. Now you wish me to rescue *you*? No, it is I whom *you* must rescue. That is why you are here. It is your own way to salvation."

"I just can't believe what you are telling me!" I retorted. "I have given years of my life to the study of money and have worked hard to attain financial success. I have thought of almost nothing else over the years. I have denied myself many things in order to become what I am today. It can't be as bad as you say."

"No, don't argue with me," my Spirit of Financial Woes replied kindly but firmly. "You have thought about money, that is true. But you have never considered the spirit of money, have you? You have trapped me away in this castle because you were afraid of me. And you have stayed far away. You have ignored me. Finally you decided to ask for help, and here you are, when I am nearly gone."

"I did not ask you for help," I said bluntly. "I have never asked other people to solve problems for me." I could not believe the pride and bitterness I heard as my voice echoed in the room.

"Oh yes, you did," the Spirit replied firmly. "The part of yourself that longs for freedom from this problem did. Trust me, I would not be here, nor would you, if you hadn't."

"Oh." I could think of nothing more to say. And then I remembered the words that had escaped as I had drifted into my inebriated unconsciousness. He was right; I had asked.

This was very confusing. Then it occurred to me, "If you say that you heard my call for help, then doesn't that mean that you are supposed to help me? Rescue me as it were?"

"Dear Avery, this is *your* journey. You will learn to help yourself. I am only here to show you where you can begin. And you begin by releasing me."

The Spirit of Financial Woes suddenly took a turn for the worse, and I knew it was the end. His breath was coming in short gasps. I could tell that he desperately wanted to finish our conversation. I leaned over to hear him. "Listen to me... carefully, Avery. Remember each... word. What I will say will help you... the rest of your journey."

He paused, and I thought perhaps I had lost him. From some place of great and deep strength, he recovered and continued haltingly and with great difficulty. "Your real issue is not... with me... not about money. I just got you here. Finally."

I thought I saw him smile a little when he said that. "Find wisdom... here. Must... understand. Learn. Be honest... need... courage."

While I sat cradling his head in my arms, the most amazing thing happened. The old man simply began to fade from my sight. I blinked rapidly to correct my vision, but it was true. His body disintegrated into millions of tiny, sparkling particles of light, leaving me holding nothing. As he disappeared, his voice called after me, "Remember this, Avery! Remember!"

Immediately after I heard the sound of clinking metal and felt on my ankles and wrists the weight of iron restraints. I knew before I looked down at myself that the chains he had worn, now bound me in his place. I had indeed rescued him, but now was trapped myself.

Chapter xvi

The old man vanished into the air, his words fading with him. My compassion for him faded just as quickly as my new reality hit me hard.

"Remember!" he had said. "Remember what?" I grumbled to myself. That he blamed me for his dire condition? That he had used me to free himself? A sour mood settled over me, and perhaps for the first time in my life, there was no escape from my feelings. There was no escape from anything.

All I knew at this moment was that I was chained to a wall in what appeared to be my very own castle in a room so deep inside of it that no one, if there were someone else in this reality, would ever hear a cry for help. Just me. Oh, yes, and my candle. OK, and the fire in the hearth—the hearth with my initials inscribed so I could not forget this was all my own doing. Great.

I looked at the candle. No, I glared at it with a vengeance. Aha! Something to blame. I wouldn't have come this far except for thinking that the candle was encouraging me. It, on the other hand, seemed to be having a great time, the flame dancing merrily. This only irritated me more.

"Oh, why don't you just go extinguish yourself somewhere? A lot of good you've done me so far!" I lashed out angrily.

Instantly I realized how lost I would feel without it, and I immediately, but reluctantly, relented. I looked over at the candle, fearing reprisal, but all I got was the sense that it was enjoying this immensely. Was it laughing at me? So much for my short-lived apology. I'd have loved to dash it to the ground, but I knew the candle still might lead me to safety. So I spared it. And myself, of course. I was still Avery Victoria Spencer, and I knew how to control my emotions especially when there was something valuable at risk.

Then my sensibility returned, and I had to laugh at myself. "You're nuts, Avery Victoria Spencer," I said aloud. "If you think a candle controls your destiny, you might as well just stay here. It would be a kindness to humanity."

There appeared to be nothing I could do about my situation, definitely a first for me. I had always had control of my life. Hadn't I? Yet it appeared that all I could do for now was to sit and wait to be rescued.

Bah! The very idea of needing to be rescued startled me out of my sullen reverie. Now was no time to blame something or someone else for my predicament. This was my castle. I would find a way out of this situation. Ha! I felt much better.

I entertained myself with 'what to do next' strategies based on some of my favorite movies and television shows. Perhaps I might be able to work some ingenious magic and release my own chains. I looked at what I had at my disposal: a candle, which meant wax and heat; my physical strength; my brilliant mind. I had tennis shoes, laces, a belt, strands of my gorgeous hair (to be used as a last resort only). How could I use them to get out of here?

My creative imagination exhausted itself with wild ideas. I still could not believe there was nothing I could do. It was such an extraordinary and heretofore unheard of experience for me. It was almost fascinating. Give me a financial investment on life support, and I could work miracles. Put me in chains in a dungeon, and I was at a loss. If only the world could see me now... Avery Victoria Spencer trapped. Imagine!

Wait a minute. Sure I was in chains, but what if they were not real? What if this place was not real? Aha! If all of this was a figment of my imagination, what then? Immediately I decided to test this idea. I got my body turned around and put my feet against the wall. Grabbing the wrist chains the best I could, I pulled with everything I had.

Real or not, the chains were as stubborn as the door to this room had been. My heart dropped when I found them to be strong and secure. Oh yes, they were medieval, but top-quality products. Nothing less would have done for my own personally-appointed dungeon. No way to undo them that I could see. No keys. No tools. I recalled the bruises I had seen on the wrists of the Spirit of Financial Woes. No use fighting and bruising my own skin.

But wait... the door. I had struggled to get it open, and it had resisted my efforts. When I quit trying, the door opened itself. What if the same rule applied here? It was worth a shot. I relaxed and let go of the chains. I looked at my wrists and my feet and tried to imagine the iron bands unlocking on their own. I waited and waited. Nothing happened. I waited some more. Then I realized that the door had opened when it was ready. It looked like I'd just have to wait for the same thing to happen here. Wait. Be patient. Let it happen when it was ready.

I wanted to make it happen. That was how I had always lived. I wanted to fight. I wanted to figure this out. I didn't care how hard it was; I wanted to be part of the solution to this problem. If I didn't do something, might I spend the rest of my life here, as my Spirit of Financial Woes had done?

It was too much to bear. I could well imagine myself here in about forty years, my hair gray and hanging unkempt over my ghostly, wrinkled face; my body, skin and bones. Yes, I had always wanted to be thin, but not that thin.

I shuddered. I'd be on the edge of death, right where I was now in this barren room and some younger, perhaps middle-aged idiot with a financial problem would show up to seek my wisdom. Ha! I'd remember how the Spirit of Financial Woes had tricked me into replacing him in the chains. I'd pull the same stunt. Ha!

Then again, if the same scenario played out, I'd have to die to be released, right? That was not, could not be the point of all this. And then the most despicable thought... someone would have to replace me as president of the bank. I couldn't bear it. I wouldn't.

The fact was that I didn't see how lying around down here was going to make me any wiser about money. If this was some sort of punishment for monetary sins, shouldn't I have lots of company? I was certain there were others far more deserving of this kind of treatment than I.

Suddenly the thoughts came racing in. I had nothing to do but think. So I did. And then I started to pay attention to my thoughts as if I had a front row seat at a play. It was as if I stepped out of my thoughts for a time and could watch them, rather than being them. It turned out to be a boring, repetitive, one-act diatribe with a petty, fickle, negative, whiny script that ran over and over and over again.

The star of the show, a woman (naturally), dressed in filthy rags, with a face full of ashes, who was hell-bent on finding something wrong with everything and everyone in the show. Who was this? Certainly not I? I always ensured a positive outcome. I never allowed a negative thought to linger in my mind.

Whoever she was, she was a masterful performer. Any challenge from a brightly dressed happy or positive thought, and the woman (whom I eventually named the 'Wicked Thought Witch') would step to center stage screaming, "How dare you interrupt me with your ridiculous pansy-assed dribble. Be gone!" while raising her trembling hand. She would point her long bony finger with wicked nails at the thought and zap it with her negative energy. Instantly the thought transformed into something ugly, with the happy thought no longer recognizable.

At the beginning of the play there had been a long line of sublime mentations waiting for their turn to challenge the Witch. As time went by, fewer and fewer of them remained. Some had been so frightened by her power that they had crawled off the stage, unwilling to face her. Wimps! Surely one of them could overcome her. I willed it to be so.

How pathetic. I was aghast. Surely this was not how my mind worked! I considered myself a positive person, always able to find something good in a situation. I never let negative circumstances get me down. Never. Shocked and appalled, I decided to intervene to make this show stop, but I was ignored. It was as if I didn't exist. Did my own mind consider me irrelevant? It was so busy with its own thoughts, its own diatribe, that I couldn't get one word (or thought) in edgewise. When had I lost control of what my mind thought about? Had I ever had control?

Over the course of time, my Wicked Thought Witch seemed to grow weary, especially as the competition thinned out and I tired of watching her. As I ceased trying to get her attention to prove her wrong, she just wore out like a balloon slowly losing its air. It was amazing.

Rather than fighting and arguing because she was obviously the master of her trade, I just let her go on without comment. I didn't fight and she lost interest. There was something strangely comforting about this process. Oh, no, I wasn't giving up and surrendering to these awful thoughts. But it was obvious that no amount of effort on my part was going to influence her, just as no amount of physical strength would break my chains and free me. So I sat and did nothing, except watch my play. At last the Wicked Thought Witch just threw up her hands and walked off the stage.

And then the most incredible thing happened. My mind became more restful and as it did so, more affirmative thoughts bubbled to the surface. While I had been focusing on the Wicked Thought Witch's performance, she had ruled the stage and my mind.

Now that I was no longer fighting for her attention—when she ceased to have an impassioned audience, it was as if the stage had been reset. Good thoughts came forward—even gratitude for things like the steady dance of my candle's flame and the fire in the hearth that provided needed warmth. The fact was that neither the candle nor the fire seemed to need to be replenished. Yes, I was grateful.

I had experienced neither hunger nor tiredness yet, and best of all, I hadn't had to go to the bathroom. Yes, these were practical blessings. Now if I could just know that gray hair wasn't beginning to appear, that I wouldn't be here for the rest of my life, I'd be content. For now. Just for this moment. Strange, I thought, to be content in this place. Was that good?

Chapter xvii

In spite of my circumstances, I had to admit I found a sense of hard, but honest, clarity in the moments that followed. I was shocked at how strange that concept was for me. There was no pressure from any outside source on how I behaved or on what I thought. Yes, the chains certainly limited my freedom of physical movement. But my mind was freer. Having become aware of what I let myself think when I wasn't paying attention, I had set about to become more aware.

Perhaps for the first time, I could examine those thoughts and make sure I really wanted to think them. No one was watching me... not my parents, the neighbors, the bank staff, the community. No one. It was like going skinny-dipping and knowing you were absolutely safe. I loved it. You didn't have to think about the horror of being found out; you could just focus on how good the water felt on your bare skin. Not that I had ever been skinny-dipping, of course. That was the other kids who did that sort of thing. But I could just imagine how it felt.

It was peaceful like that here. I could 'undress' my mind from the expectations I had learned to live with. I realized how little I had ever really paid attention to my own thoughts. Most of them, I realized, were what I thought others thought. And I had never stopped looking at what I thought they thought long enough to think about what I thought. Does that make any sense?

I realized that I had been living like a preprogrammed robot. I knew by the data I received from the body language of others, by their tone of voice, and a myriad of other receptors, just what they were thinking, which then instructed me on how I should behave.

And that was how I had lived... the way others expected me to live. Because that is how I had always felt safe and secure. But it had not been an easy way to live. Certainly it wasn't honest. My conversation with my Spirit of Financial Woes came back to me. He had mentioned the 'false and dishonorable' way I was living. This must be what he meant!

It was so clear to me now, and it was painful to realize. When different people had wanted me to behave in different ways, I had been changing who I was to suit their expectations. Was my life all an act? And was all the money I was spending part of the 'stage set' for the life I thought I was suppose to live?

In the moments that followed, my own thoughts that I had not allowed myself to think lined up like impatient customers at the complaint department. They all wanted my attention at the same time. I began hearing thoughts that I had left buried below the busy surface of my life—questions, yearnings that I had simply not acknowledged before. It was pretty intense. And noisy.

"Could each of you take a number?" I wanted to yell above the clamor. "And just shut up! Everyone will get a turn. One at a time, please!"

But my thoughts weren't buying. I knew I had to give them their way or be trampled to death. Had anyone ever died from having too many thoughts all at once? And yet these were not the negative thoughts that I had been witnessing before. These were completely different, surprisingly open and candid.

"Now look, my dear," I could hear one particularly senior thought saying, "I've been waiting longer than anyone here, and I demand to be heard!" Why did I imagine a little, old, gray-haired lady in a bold floral dress with a matching hat, white gloves, and a purple purse to match her hair?

The next shock was that none of these thoughts were about money. And suddenly I remembered the words of my Spirit of Financial Woes before he left me. He had said that my issue wasn't really about money.

Was this what he was talking about? None of the thoughts clamoring for my attention was about money, my debt, or my

financial mayhem. No, they were all about something else...
like what I really thought about things when no one else was
around. About what I valued, what I believed, what I wanted
from my life.

And it wasn't about being a bank president. Or anything
about a career. It was more than that. It was the dawning of
the realization that underneath my calm, capable, brilliantly
successful exterior, I was really a person with her own original
thoughts and opinions. It was like meeting myself for the first
time... the self that lived beneath the chaotic surface that I
thought was the real 'me.'

I had spent so much time and money creating myself in the
image of what I thought others wanted, I had forgotten who
I really was. I was proud of the life I had made for myself, but
was it really my life? Was my own self starving to death, just
like my Spirit of Financial Woes had been. Or perhaps the
Ugly Duckling was getting ready for the important task of
transformation. It was pretty interesting, having all this time on
my hands with nothing to do, no bank deals, no parties,
nothing to distract me.

So I did what I could with the time I had. I thought,
pondered, mused, meditated, and observed. I listened as
dueling opinions and emotions presented themselves. And
somehow, in the quiet place I had found inside, they all led

back to this same theme. It wasn't about the money. It was about who I really was.

Peeling back the layers of my life, it didn't take long for me to realize how strong my own self-deception had been. And the words of my Spirit of Financial Woes rang out in my head, "You suffer from the deepest form of falseness and dishonesty... so much that you do not recognize it anymore."

Incredible! I realized that I, like many others, had sized up the world at a young age and decided that the most important people in my life were not interested in anything except how I behaved. My father never asked, "Avery, what do you think about this. What would you like to do?" My mother rarely had time for leisure activities with me, never said, "Let's go shopping and buy you something you would really like to wear." It was always, "Avery, when you grow up you'll understand what I'm saying. Believe me, this is for your own good." Or, "Avery, we're going to do such and so." Or, "Avery, I know you'd rather have something prettier, but we can't afford it."

Do not get me wrong. My parents did everything they could for me, but it was all based on their values and opinions. So, when I grew up I simply transferred my habit of substituting the values and opinions of others for my own. It never occurred to me that mine mattered. I honestly believed that I didn't count... that what other people thought about me was more important than what I thought about myself. I had never considered my own opinion. Their likes and dislikes, their preferences, were all-important. All I had ever wanted to do in life was to be liked and to be safe.

Of course, living like this kept me busy trying to find my way through the endless maze of human relationships. No wonder I didn't want anyone in my personal life. I had literally 'spent' myself into being what I thought would be acceptable to others, ignoring my own thoughts and feelings. I could not bear the influence of another human being in my personal space. I lived and slept alone and gladly. A life 'all to myself.'

The only significant change about being grown up was that there was no one to say 'No' to me anymore, at least about what I spent my money on. So I said 'Yes' to everything I wanted or thought I wanted. I shopped and bought to satisfy the angry little girl inside who could never have what she craved, could never wear anything fashionable or remotely trendy, who was so tired of the words 'No, we can't afford it.' But I realized now that even my spending was about preserving the image that I wanted the world to have of me and not about who I was or what I wanted.

As I half-sat, half-lay against the unyielding stone wall, I watched the fire burning steadily and strongly. Then I remembered my candle. I had been ignoring it, too busy with my own thoughts to give it any attention. Half-apologetically, I reached to encircle it in my embrace. Its flame seemed to smile reassuringly at me, forgiving me. Obviously happy to be with me and pleased with my progress.

I wondered how the candle kept burning and never melted; I wondered how the fire in the hearth kept going. What did they represent? That someone or something was taking care of me? If so, who or what? It was reassuring, if nothing else. Slowly, I began to relax. Then I began to get sleepy. For the first time, since coming to this place of mystery, I slept.

Chapter xviii

$\mathcal{I}$ awoke to a sense of brightness and warmth all around me. "Ah," I thought, as I lay quietly musing before consciousness completely overtook me, "I have just been dreaming all of this." I felt the great relief of one who awakens after a particularly bad dream—to realize gratefully that it was just a story playing out in one's unconscious mind. I took a deep breath and began a lazy, relaxed stretch. The chains biting into my wrists jerked me back into reality, the pain of overreaching my bonds confirming that I had not been dreaming.

In spite of all the learning of the prior day, my anger at my inability to do anything about my circumstances was my first emotion of the new day. I sat up, stiff and uncomfortable, shackled in the same old dungeon-like room, alone as before. I reached awkwardly for my candle. It had kept right on burning while I slept.

Except for that small gratitude, my bravery and courage were all used up. Without the grit I was known for to sustain me, the realization that my life was a sham had sent shockwaves through my psyche. I could feel vast emotional chasms shifting and splitting inside me. Dammed up for years, they broke now with a force that I could not begin to control. I wept.

Which would be putting what I was doing mildly. Actually, I wailed, moaned, and raged. I thrashed as much as my chains would permit. It was not pretty.

No one would ever call me a crybaby. I never cried. It was such a weak, female thing to do. I didn't even really know how to cry, and sometimes I felt terrible when it would be an appropriate emotion, but I couldn't feel it—like at my mother's wake and funeral. No, I had conquered every situation in my life like a real soldier. Until now.

Deep sobs tore loose within me and exploded into the empty room. Choking and gasping, I could hear the sound echo and ricochet until I felt as if there were a chorus of women weeping with me. Which I resented. I did not want to weep. Only weak women wept, and I was not one of them. Which just made me feel even more like crying. Damn! Damn! Damn!

So I cried and swore and cried and swore until I could cry no more and cursing could no longer express my pain. I swam through agony and grief, pain and sorrow and aching despair until at last I reached the other side of the ocean of tears. I flung what was left of myself onto the beach of emptiness, and was surprised to discover a restful place of comfort and quiet. I had never been here before. I had not known the sweet release of tears until now. I was amazed at the sense of repose and utter calm.

Finally drying my tears on my shirt sleeve, I opened my aching eyes. I could not believe what I saw. All around me lay tiny sparkling tear-shaped diamonds as if each tear had become a valuable treasure.

I had to smile in spite of myself, encouraged that by releasing my sorrow, something so beautiful had been created. I ran my fingers over them gently. It was so ironic. Here, where diamonds were of no use to me, they abounded. In my other life, where I could really use them to pay off my debts, I did not have even one. Laughing, I glanced at my candle, certain that its flame was dancing brighter than ever, as if we were enjoying the joke together.

Breathing deeply, I was now able to understand more clearly, as if my tears had washed away useless old perceptions. What a gift, I realized, to meet my Spirit of Financial Woes, even if I hadn't liked what he had to say. I was glad that I was chained... that I couldn't run away from this process. I couldn't busy myself with other things and take my mind off it. I couldn't just go shopping! And I laughed out loud again. What a familiar escape shopping had been, and how ludicrous. Spending money I didn't have to make myself feel better about myself and my horrible financial situation. I laughed and laughed—another real, from-the-gut feeling. Honest. Clean. Genuine.

I sat thoughtfully, gazing into the fire, completely at peace.

Chapter xix

It was at that moment that the flames seemed to grow bolder and brighter, clustering together so that they formed an image. I rubbed my eyes, certain that I was hallucinating. Try as I might to dispel it, the image refused to go away. Suddenly a figure stepped out of the fire in the hearth and into the room and began to walk toward me. I was almost too frightened to look, but of course I did. I could not take my eyes off her. I lack the words to fully describe the brilliance of her beauty, but I will attempt to share what I saw.

She was surrounded by radiant light, as if the sun walked with her into the dark room. Her hair was a brilliant orange-red, the color of the flames that burned endlessly in the hearth. It flowed around her head, long and wavy, and stood out like the rays of the sun. Her slim figure was clothed in a gorgeous gown of deep royal purple and shimmering gold. Her left shoulder was draped in the royal purple, the right shoulder in gold. The two colors crisscrossed in the bodice and then wrapped around her lovely body, entwining her in spiraling splendor. A royal purple cape was clasped at each shoulder with a golden brooch. Lined in the same shimmering gold as her dress, her cape flowed gracefully behind her toward the hearth. I no longer could tell where her cape ended and the fireplace began.

She wore a simple and beautiful necklace around her throat. Three strands of white pearls met on each side of what I recognized immediately as the image of the winged swan. It appeared to be made of a solid diamond, with the swan's beak, eyes, and fanned wing tips etched in gold. It rested quietly in the hollow of her throat.

A tiara of small diamonds rested on her head, the swan crest creating a crowning touch in the center. The diamonds immediately reminded me of the tears I had recently shed. I glanced around at the stone floor and realized that the diamonds were gone. Was she wearing my tears as an exquisite crown? The thought stunned me and warmed my heart at the same time. She was simplicity, beauty, and refined grace—a goddess. As she walked gracefully toward me, her radiance lit the way.

Even before I knew what she represented, I understood that my mysterious visitor was another spirit guide, meant to take me further on my journey. May I be so honest as to admit how much more enthralled I was to encounter her than I had been the Spirit of Financial Woes? Who would blame me?

I hesitated to speak, as if words penetrating the air might cause this moment to explode. But I heard myself addressing her, compelled by some force I could not understand. "Who are you, My Lady?" I implored quietly but eagerly. Because of my bonds, I could not bow or curtsy, but I lowered my head reverently. She did not answer immediately, but came and stood before me. Then she knelt by my side, and I felt her hands gently lifting my chin and then she looked at me. Our eyes met and I felt her strength and energy reach deep into my soul.

"Avery Victoria Spencer, who do you think I am?" she responded in a quiet voice, barely above a whisper. As she continued to look directly into my eyes, her own were deep pools of intense love, warmth, and wisdom that invited me into clarity and knowing. I could not resist. She smiled, and there could not possibly be anything wrong in the world.

"I don't know who you are, My Lady," I protested. "The Virgin Mary?" I felt a bit stupid saying it, but it was the only thing that came to my mind.

She smiled so gently and laughed so softly I could not help but feel loved. Shaking her head side to side, she said nothing. Silence consumed the room, and I ached for it to be filled.

I could not bear to let the conversation end. "I do not know who you are, My Lady," I confessed honestly. "I only know that you are here and that you have come to take me further on this journey, to teach me what I need to know. I am humbled to be in your presence."

Continuing to smile, she beckoned me as she rose gracefully and stood in front of me. "Yes. That is enough for now. Come with me," she said. "We have much to discuss." Enthralled, I started to rise and suddenly remembered my chains.

I froze in place. "I cannot, My Lady," I said sadly. "I sit here chained by my own stupidity."

"Ah," she said, as if to tease me only slightly, but with great love. "And if your own stupidity has placed you in chains, cannot your own wisdom release you?"

"I do not know," I answered her. But in that moment, the question she asked was answered in my mind. And I knew, as I had failed to recognize before, that indeed, I was in these chains of my own making. Certainly I could release them!

Empowered by her presence in the room, energy and confidence surged through me as my familiar old bravado returned. I was Avery Victoria Spencer, and I could do this! I tried to stand, to walk toward her, but the chains held me tight. I struggled, certain that I could overcome them, but to no avail. I knew I looked like a fool, and I sank to the floor in grief and humiliation.

Chapter xx

Turning to implore her help, I saw that she was gone. I cursed and swore bitterly, thinking I had lost her. Why had she come? What had caused her to leave? Why in the moment of my most profound need did she leave me, just as the Spirit of Financial Woes had? For the first time, I noticed the fire in the hearth diminished, as if she had taken the warmth and the intensity of the fire with her as she left.

Reaching for my candle, I heaved it across the room where it fell with a sickening thud far out of my reach. "I hate you!" I declared. "This is all your fault!" And then I let rage such as I had never known consume me. All my life I had 'sucked it in' when it came to disappointment and broken promises. I suddenly remembered all the times I had been overlooked as if I didn't exist. All the years I had struggled to come up with ways to feel accepted and worthy, the almost insurmountable hurdles I had overcome to make my own way in the world. All of the memories seemed to boil over inside me.

"Why had I always had to do things for myself?" I thought bitterly. Why was it always so difficult? Why didn't anyone ever reach out to help me? Well, OK, maybe Evelyn did, and sure my parents a little, but otherwise, I had created and endured everything, alone. Was it to be no different here where spirit guides came and went and left me to deal with my own issues? I was tired of the burdens of my life, of carrying them alone. It was not fair, and I was pissed.

There was no one here to care how I behaved. There was no one here to see or hear, so I gave in to my feelings. I kicked and screamed and cursed. I pulled against my chains with all my angry strength. I felt superhuman, like all the unfairness and misery of my lifetime had built up to channel its torturous energy through me. Surely I could break out of here.

"I don't need you!" I screamed to no one.

Once again, my efforts were in vain. The fact was that surely I could not. I strained against this physical manifestation of my financial prison with every ounce of strength I had and gasped as I felt it ebb out of me, all used up. I was exhausted—physically and emotionally spent. I sank to the floor. And all I had to show for it now were some bruises on my wrists and ankles. I rubbed them thoughtfully.

Then I remembered that my own Spirit of Financial Woes had done the same thing. I recalled the etched markings on his own wasted frame that showed how he had struggled against his captivity. Surely he felt this same rage as he watched me strengthen the chains of my financial confinement and his. He was powerless to stop me. Or help me. Until I asked.

"Remember," he had said as he disappeared. "Remember."

He had said that all of this was an answer to my cry for help. Was he suggesting that I should appreciate this torturous experience? Chained in this dungeon where I could do nothing about my situation, I questioned the wisdom of asking. I had never felt so helpless. I would rather fight to my last breath to overcome something on my own than ask for help. Asking was tantamount to admitting that I was weak, incapable, or afraid. It put others in control of my experience. I despised helplessness. And I did not accept it in my life. Not even now.

And yet there had been progress. I had begun to see things in a new way. I realized that each time I tried to 'do something' to free myself, I failed. Nothing I was doing had done any good. And it never had, really. All of my efforts to improve the financial circumstances of my life had thus far come to naught. And in that moment, when I realized I could not, in any imaginable way, get myself out of this situation through my own efforts, I gave up.

No, it was not giving up; it was more like surrendering, letting go to something else perhaps. It was not with a resigned attitude that my heart raised its white flag. It was with a spirit of expectancy and hope. What I could not do of my own efforts, still could be done. I was sure of that. But I needed help.

"OK," I said out loud. "I understand. I am ready to receive your aid, dear spirit. Return to me when you will."

I sat patiently now, expectantly. I knew only this—the negative emotions that I had experienced would never resolve my issues, nor could they ever liberate me. What a profound moment that was!

Suddenly and with great horror, I remembered my candle, and my eyes and heart went searching for it. Ah, there it was, off in the distance and far from my reach, standing upright, its flame bright, steady, and true. With gratitude, I breathed deeply and gave in to the calm that was waiting for me. I knew that the answers to my questions were in the quiet, not in the clamor, of my emotions.

Chapter xxi

"I believe you misplaced this," she stood once again before me, holding my candle out to me. I accepted it gratefully and examined it closely, checking for any bruises I might have inflicted on it. I saw nothing; no damage anywhere. Amazing.

Looking up at the spirit guide, I smiled and suddenly I was laughing at the episode she must have witnessed. She joined me with her soft, gentle laugh, the kind that healed and blessed.

"Thank you for returning to me," I said. "I think I am ready for you now."

"Yes, dear Avery, while I am always with you, you sense me only when you call me from a place of possibility and wonder, not from effort or egotistical frenzy," the spirit guide explained quietly.

"I know you think that I left you, but, dear Avery..." she paused. Her next words burned into my very soul. "It is you who leave me in those moments when you are relying on your own superficial efforts. I am always with you; I simply wait for your return to me."

She stood beside me and repeated the question she had asked before. "And now," she said, as if no time had intervened, "if these chains are of your own making, why cannot you release yourself from them?"

This time, I understood that the question was not intended as a challenge by which I was to prove myself, but as an evocative statement—to teach me to look deeper.

I raised my chained arms out to her. "Teach me about this," I implored her. "You are here to help guide me on my journey. I do not know how to free myself of these chains, but you do. Teach me. Answer the questions that lie so deep in my soul I hardly know how to ask them."

As I watched with fascination, she knelt beside me and lightly touched each of my wrists and ankles. One by one, the huge heavy iron shackles fell off and clanked to the floor. I was free! As if to prove a greater point, she took each of my bruised ankles and wrists, one at a time, into one hand and waved her other hand over each of them. They were completely healed.

As I knelt in reverence and awe before her, full of deep gratitude, she rebuked me gently, saying, "It is you who allowed me to release these chains. You have allowed me to do so because you believe in me. You will see that you have the power to free yourself when you begin to believe in yourself. But come," she said, "there is much for us to discuss. You are ready."

Chapter xxii

She took my hand. I followed her toward a door that I had not seen before. I was starting to get the idea that in this magical place, things happened when it was time to see them and not before.

Suddenly remembering my candle, I glanced back at it, wondering whether I should take it with me. But its bubbly glow encouraged me. "Go without me," it seemed to say. "I'll be fine. But no more launching me across the room, OK?" I smiled apologetically and left the room. I was in the hands of a new guide, and I could not wait to learn what she had to tell me.

We entered a quiet, wonderful patio garden where a table set for two awaited us. Because I had just come from a dark, cold chamber with almost no light, the intense, warm sunshine blinded me momentarily. When I could finally open my watering eyes, I gazed around me, stunned by the beauty. My senses could hardly absorb the wonder and yet I drank it in deeply and gratefully.

I could see that the castle—my castle—was set near the edge of a cliff, overlooking the sea. Far below, a ship sailed out of a harbor, its sails full and taut. The water sparkled as if the stars from the previous night had fallen into the water—an illusion created by the sunlight dancing on its surface. Turning away from the majestic scene, I was stunned by the breathtaking beauty of the forested and snow-capped mountains in the background.

The castle itself was an amazing site to behold. Standing tall and regal, I was certain it could be seen for miles. A proper medieval fortress, with more turrets and towers than I could count, it would be virtually impossible to be surprised by an attack of any kind here.

A flag flew from each one of the conical roofs of the towers, high and proud. As each one responded to the gentle breeze, I saw over and over, on their white background, my royal crest. It was unimaginable that all this was mine, and yet I was its prisoner. That thought reminded me of the spirit guide who was sitting quietly while I took in my surroundings. I could not believe such beauty existed in my own imagination (or wherever I was).

I walked back to the table noticing that the patio garden was obviously old and well-tended. Rather than being overrun with plants, simple clusters of delphiniums, foxglove, and lavender grew here and there. Purple clematis climbed along the beams of the arbor overhead that hung heavily laden with almost-ripe pears. Not overdone or obsessively manicured like my own garden at home, but simple and elegant. And here and there, roses of several different varieties bloomed fragrantly.

My place was set to the side of the spirit guide, rather than across from her. Ah, a familiar strategy from my banking days. Across from the other party was oppositional; authoritative. Next to the person, on the perpendicular side of the table was the position of cooperation and openness.

As I took my seat, I could feel the heat of the sun-soaked stone floor penetrating through my tennis shoes. I had an irresistible urge to remove them and let the warmth absorb into my feet and legs. Immediately, my wish was granted, and somehow my shoes lay on the flagstones beside my feet.

There was such peace and quiet here. The sound of baroque music cascaded softly over our heads from an open window above us in the castle. I saw no other people.

Chapter xxiii

The spirit guide took my hands in hers and spoke quietly. "You came on this journey because of your burden of financial woes. You have thought that you were on a journey to understand money," she said and then hesitated. Accurate enough, I thought. I implored her to continue.

"As the Spirit of Financial Woes explained to you, the real message of this journey is not about money at all but something far, far more important. Your obsession with money exists on a superficial level and is simply a tool meant to draw you deeper into your wisdom where the true gift of the message of this burden awaits you. It is often necessary for humans to be given challenges or 'essential burdens' as we call them, to help them identify where they have been distracted from their 'true selves,' their purpose... their greatness.

"This is true of any type of obsession that you cannot overcome. This 'essential burden' is a gift, and it has a message. This gift's purpose is to remind you who you really are and to bring you back to your glorious, wise, 'true self.'

"It happens that your 'essential burden' is money. For many people, money works as the burden to draw them back to their hearts. These issues are meant to be like compass readings when we have wandered too far from our path. When we have forgotten our greatness. I hope that you can see, here in this place, that money is completely and utterly irrelevant. It is not the reason you are here. Do you begin to understand?"

I nodded. Much of what she was saying to me reminded me of the thoughts I had been thinking while in the dungeon. I had gotten far enough on my own to realize that there was something wrong with the financial foundation on which I had built my life. That false foundation and sense of security had already been shattered. I had only just begun to consider that my life to this point had been built on a false premise.

But more than that, my thoughts stopped at the word she had used twice now: *greatness*. It struck the very core of my soul and exploded, spreading warmth throughout my entire being. I had goose bumps. I longed to know more. This concept of greatness, of learning about my 'true self,' felt like the beginning of a new foundation. A better, stronger, solid one—the right one.

In getting distracted into a life that now felt amazingly irrelevant to me, I was missing a true sense of the wonder of who I was. I had never thought of that. And if it was true that there was greatness inside of me, certainly that meant that there was something I needed to do now to re-create my life.

The spirit guide had been silent during my musings. Now she smiled at me and squeezed my hands gently as if to bring me back to her and to emphasize what she was going to say. I understood instinctively that she knew what I was thinking.

"Be careful here," she warned with gentle concern. "You keep wanting to have something to work on—something to *do*. And that is not what we are talking about. You have nothing to work on, but you do have something inside of you that wants to be expressed. There's a big difference between the two. Can you see that?"

I could not say for certain that I did. Something had not felt right for a long time. Now I sensed what that 'something' was; it was my 'essential self,' my greatness, gently asking for my attention. OK, perhaps not gently.

It was all falling into place. In spite of that, I wasn't all that certain that I liked everything she was saying. If I didn't have to work to change something, then what? Not working on something felt empty to me. Nothing in my life had ever 'just happened.' I had always expended tremendous effort and overcome incredible obstacles to accomplish my goals. Clearly there was more to learn.

As I thought about this, I noticed that somehow food and drink had arrived. No people. Just the food, instantly, and just what I wanted to eat. Now, for the first time, I was hungry. Thankfully, it was not extravagant fare, just a platter of my favorite fresh fruits and cheeses.

I took a delicate sip of pure water from the simple crystal goblet that had been placed in front of me and couldn't avoid noticing my royal crest etched in its smooth surface. And then I began to eat. While I couldn't wait to taste everything on my plate, I did not want to gorge myself or behave inappropriately in front of this exotic guide whom I had decided to call "The Spirit of Greatness," but restraint was difficult. She watched silently while I ate. After a few moments, I spoke.

Chapter xxiv

"If I understand you, and I believe I do, frustration with superficial things and the problems I have experienced with money are messengers to tell me that I am 'off course' in my life... that I am not doing or expressing something deep within me that wants to be experienced. I assume 'greatness' is that something.

"But I am not sure what it is. I have never considered the possibility of something 'great' being part of my life. You know that I have been contemplating my life—what I have created myself to be—and wondering whether what I have created is really what I am meant to be, or more important, what I want to be."

"Good," she said, smiling and clapping her hands gently, keeping the heels of the palms together as if she were at a golf tournament. "You have begun to understand."

Only begun, I thought? After all I have been through, I've only just begun? Oops... I caught myself quickly, took a deep breath, and returned to the process at hand.

"It is not about the money," she said. "It has never been about money."

Then she went on. "Your life is so much more than that...
things much bigger and more far-reaching. The purpose of this
visit is to refocus your attention on who you really are, and from
that understanding, allow you to live your life more fully. Your
problems with money will heal themselves as you discover your
greatness. I am here, you are here, because you have asked for help
with this. What you are experiencing is your own wisdom
speaking to you. Does that make sense?"

I frowned. No, it did not make sense yet, anything was
possible. She went on.

"The beginning of this process for all individuals is to
recognize that they cannot overcome their 'essential burdens'
through their own efforts. They have tried and failed enough
that they come to a point of giving up. And yet, it is not giving
up, but surrendering to another possibility. It is important that
they do not yield to the temptation of despair and resign
themselves to their fate. As you have learned, the 'giving up' is
really surrendering—it is being willing to fall into the arms of
who you really are. The way to do this is by listening to your
own wisdom as you are doing at this moment.

"For some, the journey is short from the realization of the
burden to the wisdom of its message. For others, it is a long
journey, and for some, the journey is not taken in just one
lifetime. You have reached this important point in your

relationship with money and with your 'essential' self. You have asked for help from the source of all wisdom, which is within you.

"This is the beginning of the most important journey of your life—the journey to learn what lies within you and longs to be expressed. This is the journey to your own wisdom. I am a physical manifestation of the 'greatness' that lies within you, as it does in every person."

Wow, I thought. I just couldn't get over it. There is greatness inside of me? Wow! More goose bumps.

Chapter xxv

he Spirit of Greatness smiled and continued. "Consider this. If your superficial desire for money were satisfied, then what? If accumulating money really were your only goal in life—and it certainly appears to have been that way—and you accomplish that goal, then what? And what happens if you don't?

"Do you see how empty it all is? What meaning does this ambition for money really give your life, whether you accomplish it or not? The quest for money is not the purpose of your life, nor does it contain the answer to your questions. It is only meant to draw you deeper into your true self.

"Always remember this: Money is meant to follow, never to lead, in life. Allowing money to lead is where the expression the 'love of money is the root of all evil' comes from. Obsession with money leads us to evil because it leads us away from who we really are—our greatness. Whatever leads us away from our greatness is evil. Do you understand this?" (Oh, did I!)

"You have thought that when you focused on having money, your life would get better. It does not work that way.

Life is not about money... or any of the other superficial obsessions to which we cling. It is so much more. Focus on the 'more' of life, and a proper relationship with money will follow."

I was taking all of this into my starving soul and basking in the light of truth that was beginning to dawn.

The Spirit of Greatness paused while I absorbed these concepts, and then went on. "In the same way that your issues with money are not about money, the debt that chains you is not the money debt that you so abhor. That is simply a physical manifestation of the true debt you are experiencing within yourself. The world you know on the surface of your life, the insurmountable issues you face, are just mirrors that reflect inner truth to you. Do you know what the true 'debt' is here?"

I nodded. I knew that we had reached the truth and my core issue. I could feel the walls around my life beginning to collapse as the foundation shifted. Underneath the issue of money was a deeper and greater need. And I was quite sure that I knew what the debt was... I was in debt to myself. I owed myself the opportunity to express what was truly within me, what I truly wanted to do with my life. I had the concept, but the idea of what that might be was too much to bear. It frightened me.

While I'd like to say that I just 'got it all' and my life changed instantly, something snapped within me. Too much was happening all at once. The life I had set myself up to live now felt empty and false. Life as I had lived it was over, but I wasn't sure yet what would replace it. 'Greatness,' of course, but I didn't know what that meant.

The vulnerability was too much for me—as the foundation of my life was pulled out from under me, there was nothing solid to replace it. I was dangling between life as I had lived it and life as I would live it in the future. It troubled me to think that I could get this far and still not know where to go from here. But the pieces were literally beginning to fall into place. I wanted nothing more than to move on to the next step. Quickly, so I wouldn't be afraid.

Chapter xxvi

"How do I find my purpose—or express my greatness, as you say?" I asked. I fought to stay with the spirit of the thought and not let my anxiousness show, which was nonsense because the Spirit of Greatness knew anyway.

She knew I was having trouble staying with her now. I wanted nothing more than to run away from this. It was too much. I was losing my connection to her. Still, I went on; I knew I had to get through this part, no matter how clumsily or fearfully. I had to say the next part.

"Is it possible that I will not find, I mean never express, this greatness in my life?" As I spoke, I began to realize the depth of this question. I was afraid of this as nothing else. This was indeed the real and true issue.

Money had been a mask to my real fear. Now removed, I knew it had camouflaged an immense void. Like an exposed nerve, the pain was unbearable, and I longed to cover it up again, to get a firm foundation under me, to stop this free-fall. I felt that I had to know what this 'greatness' meant for me, personally, or I would go crazy.

"I think that deep inside of me I know that I have not found my greatness, or at least I have not heeded it. And I now know that what I fear the most is missing it, never expressing it. Or maybe I am afraid to express it. I don't know," I ended with a sob in my throat. Oh, great, tears again.

I realized that I had not even drawn a breath as the realizations escaped from my lips. I looked to my Spirit of Greatness for reassurance, but she was fading from my sight. I was not surprised this time.

"Don't leave me!" I called piteously after her. Yet I knew that she had been right earlier when she said she was not leaving me. I was leaving her. Having met my own Spirit of Greatness, I did not want to go on from this moment without her. And yet, I could no longer bear the light of her truth.

Chapter xxvii

My mind whirled, and I was back in my old, now-familiar dungeon. Yes, the chains were back on. I struggled with the new discovery. I became angry and frustrated with the Spirit of Greatness.

"Why won't you stay with me when I need comfort?" I begged. I spoke aloud fearfully and rapidly, but to no one, since she had already vanished. I was alone again, with only my candle.

"Why will you only speak to me when I am still and quiet? Why, when I am struggling, do you go away?" I was talking louder and louder as the frustration grew.

"Can't you help me as I work through these questions? Tell me why my thinking is wrong. Challenge me! Help me! Don't desert me! I feel like I am so close to the truth I seek! You speak of my greatness as being what I should focus on, and that I do not need to do anything about it. Yet surely I must do something to create it. Or allow it to come forth. I want to understand. You are not playing fair!"

One thing about yelling in a big empty room is that you get to hear the sound of what you have just said as it echoes back to you. I realized what was happening and I had to smile. Anger and self-pity had rushed to my rescue again, but these feelings wouldn't help answer the questions that were ricocheting around in my mind. "Be gone!" I ordered the anxious feelings. And then I sat down to rest and to become quiet again.

As I slipped deep into thought, I considered once again why the Spirit of Greatness would not stand up against my honest fear and questioning. I knew she was not timid or afraid. Her entire being radiated beauty, wisdom, courage, and strength. No, it was not because she was intimidated. And I had to laugh at the very thought of the Spirit of Greatness cowering in front of anything.

No, there was a reason she would not take on the challenge, and as I focused my attention quietly on this matter, I heard a voice say, "Because the answers do not lie within your fear."

Turning my head, I thought the Spirit of Greatness had come back into the room to rescue me now that I had become quieter. But there was no one there. The voice was my own, my own wisdom speaking to me. The Spirit of My Own Greatness.

I continued the contemplation aloud. "What my spirit knows never needs to be defended, argued with, or put into debate against fear. That is what faith is—the deep, quiet knowing that nothing can alter."

Thoughts flowed effortlessly from deep inside me. I realized that every time I became anxious, worried, and full of fear, the clamor in my head took over so that I could not hear my own self. That whenever that happened, I left my voice of wisdom behind. All I needed to do was to return to the quiet. Sometimes that was the hardest thing to do, because it felt the same as doing nothing.

The Spirit of Greatness was right. It wasn't that my wisdom ever left. I just couldn't find my way to it through my negative emotions. My only task, at those times, was to become quiet and to listen. Be quiet and breathe. That was all. The wisdom would be waiting for me.

The fire in the hearth blazed. The flame of the candle beside me seemed to dance with delight. I was weary, but content. I settled back and fell into a deep sleep.

Chapter xxviii

Or at least I think I slept. As I drifted toward unconsciousness, I thought I heard someone laughing. But I could not rouse interest long enough to wake up. I drifted deeper and deeper into slumber, hardly noticing that the laughter was getting louder. I was too tired to care. Even a cold stone floor could not diminish my desire to sleep.

It took me a minute to realize that I was not sleeping at all, but standing at the entrance of a long, long corridor in the castle, one that seemed to go on forever into the darkness. My candle had accompanied me on the trip, and as I looked down at it in my hands, it struck me that I was free of my chains. I had no idea how they had come off. I hadn't done anything consciously to remove them. But it was an encouraging sign. They were ready to release me. I turned my attention to the hallway.

Along the outside stone wall as far as I could see there were tall windows, draped in elegantly rich gold and purple crisscrossing fabric swags that fell gracefully to the floor where they puddled perfectly. The brass valance rods also swagged and then crested to the center of each window where the image of a swan pulled the glorious, rich intertwining fabrics to a peak. George, my decorator, would have been proud.

As I looked across the hall, I saw doors—heavy, dark doors—all closed but leading, I presumed, into more rooms in the castle. Perhaps bedrooms, I imagined, or sitting rooms, parlors, or an immense ballroom.

The doors were evenly spaced across from the beautifully draped windows. As I began to walk down the hallway, I noted that all the doors were identical. How one would ever find the right room here was beyond me. I could almost hear a butler saying, "And your room, madam, is the fifty-second door on the right." Right.

I stared intently at the door closest to me. Above it, I noticed my royal crest once again. The door was crafted similarly to the door that had opened into the dungeon, with six boards banded together, but this time, with intricate iron scrollwork that held them together. The scrollwork was incredibly designed into spiraling, winding, and twining vines across the door. Looking more closely I saw that even the lever door handle was engraved with my emblem. There could be no doubt that this was where I was supposed to be.

I stood there, puzzled, but curious and excited. I decided to open the door closest to me and placed my hand on the latch to do so. I pressed it and pushed gently to open the door. But, like the door to the dungeon, it did not budge. I knew better than to try to open it myself. I knocked and waited. But there was no answer.

I moved down the hall to the next one, thinking that one of them should open for me. This was my castle, wasn't it? If the doors belonged to me, why couldn't I open them? There was no need to answer that question.

Chapter xxix

My efforts were interrupted by the sound of the laughter that had drawn me to this place. I had forgotten about that. Now hearing it again, I was certain the sound was coming closer. I was tempted to run in the other direction, but only for an instant. Running away in fear seemed foolish if this was my castle, and there was a purpose for which I was here. I took a deep breath and let go of my apprehension, realizing that when I did so, I was actually flooded with curiosity, excited and fascinated by what might lie ahead.

As I peered far down the corridor into the darkness, I noticed a small, golden light beginning to appear. As it moved closer, I could hear not only the laughing, which had turned into a merry tune, but a jingling sound, like bells at holiday time. And, humming, perhaps? I cocked my ear toward the sound to see if I could get a better sense of it. It was so dark at the other end of the corridor that, for a time, all I could see was the bright, happy little light. And all I could hear were the sounds of jingling and laughter, and humming, coming closer and closer.

Someone was having a good time, but I glanced tentatively at my candle to get a read on its reaction to what was occurring. It was almost vibrating with joy. I couldn't help but be intrigued.

At last, I began to make out a figure, certainly not the gorgeous and serene Spirit of Greatness I had met earlier, but this time, a sprightly little person... a man, I thought. Not given to a stately gait, this figure fairly danced and skipped toward me down the corridor. My intrigue soon turned to disappointment.

"Ridiculous." That was the first word that came to my mind. What spirit could this be? Certainly not of the same dignity and grace of my last visitor. I viewed this one with a touch of disdain. Grown-up people who made fools of themselves did not impress me. I had no idea what lesson this character might be coming to teach me.

"Avery Victoria Spencer, you've come at last!" the merry stranger exclaimed when he finally reached me moments later. He bowed comically and offered me his candle. His was different from mine; it was a white taper affair that sat in a golden candlestick holder complete with a finger ring for holding. However, his candle bore the swan emblem, just as mine did.

I grasped the candle, trying to take in what I saw before me, my hands completely occupied by candles, his and mine. I could accept the skeletal, impoverished image of my Spirit of Financial Woes and the elegant, radiant image of my Spirit of Greatness as being expressions of myself. This spirit would be a challenge.

The color of his clothing was the same as the Spirit of Greatness—deep royal purple and gold, the fabric, pure velvet. But that was all that was similar between them.

Instead of being elegantly attired, he was dressed as a court jester. His silly hat had three collapsed cones sticking out from the center, each tasseled with tiny bells—hence the jingling sound I had heard.

His torso was covered in a purple and gold striped tutu-looking affair except that it ballooned at his waist and bubbled down to the top of each leg. To add to the charade, where his costume ended, he was dressed in tights, one gold leg and one purple leg.

The grand finale to this outfit was on his feet. They were covered in huge, preposterous purple and gold slippers, the purple on the outside of the shoe, the gold on the inside, front to back. Each had a buckle on top, made of precious, sparkling jewels. The toe of each slipper curled over at the top and had, yes, a tiny bell dangling from it.

He must have noticed me staring, because just at that moment, he wiggled his toes and made the bells jangle. And then he began dancing and humming merrily, as if he were possessed with joy and merriment. He pranced around in front of me, unable to stand still. I couldn't help but smile even if I thought he looked ridiculous. He noticed my smile immediately.

"Oh, you're smiling!" he exclaimed, clapping his hands gaily after putting his palms together, just as the Spirit of Greatness had done. His face was merry and bright. His eyes twinkled—welcoming, inviting me to look deeply into them to a place where I was certain I could know everything, a place I was certain I had never been before. It was impossible to imagine anything but a smile on his face. He was obviously just so pleased with himself that he couldn't stand it. As though getting me to smile were an accomplishment.

Still recovering from a deeply contemplative session, I was hardly prepared for this hilarity. That did not seem to matter to this guy. In fact, on the contrary, it seemed to rather amuse him.

Chapter xxx

"My dear Avery Victoria," he exclaimed with so much genuine enthusiasm I could not help but be drawn in. "I am so glad to see you have arrived at last! Do you recognize me?"

I hardly knew how to respond, but I decided no guessing games. Why did each of these spirit guides think I should know who they were? I really hated not knowing, which is probably why I rarely let myself get put into a situation where I didn't. But I was learning to tell the truth.

"No, not really," I replied simply and waited for his response.

"Oh?" he exclaimed and then added, "I'm not surprised!" At this point, he burst out laughing.

Before I could catch myself, I snapped, "What's so funny?" Gasping in horror, I braced myself expecting that he would disappear and that I would be put back in chains.

But instead of disappearing because of my negative response, he reacted by going into an amazing contortion, such as I could never have imagined. His head started spinning around and around, setting the bells on his hat clamoring. As his head was spinning, his eyeballs appeared to pop out of his head simply in response to the increasing velocity of his head spin. His ears began to stretch and get longer, and I had to jump back in order not to be pummeled by them as they whipped by me. His smiling lips literally wrapped around his entire head. As if to punctuate his merriment, a spray of something golden that appeared like tiny stars shot out the top of his head, lifting his hat high into the air.

I stared at this spectacle in complete amazement and could not help smiling a little in spite of myself. In fact, it seemed to tap into an undiscovered reservoir of hilarity someplace inside of me and pulled it out into the room. First, chuckling, and then gut-wrenching, unstoppable laughter.

Feeling suddenly free to enjoy his silliness, I collapsed, weeping with laughter at the scene in front of me. I gave up trying to hold on to the candles. Setting them down beside me, I gave in to the comical scene. How long had it been since I had done that? Had I ever?

My laughter seemed to bring him back to himself. Like the end of the Tilt-A-Whirl at the fair, everything started to slow down. His head began to steady while his hat fell back into place, sliding down over his face. At that moment both his head and face came to a screeching halt, only now they were backwards. I tapped his shoulder, giggling like a seven-year old. His head quickly spun 180 degrees to look at me. At least he was aligned correctly again.

"Whew! That was exciting!" he said, moving his lips that still surrounded his entire head. This 'surround smile' continued to beam as he readjusted his eyes and ears, which was no small undertaking.

First, he had to literally pick up the ends of his long ears and put them back in position. This he did by pulling them out even farther and then quickly releasing them. Much like the retractable cord on a vacuum cleaner—his ears snapped back into place. Did it hurt? I wondered. Apparently not.

To readjust his eyes, he put his fists one to either side of his face close where his eyes belonged and by 'cranking' them at the same time, he appeared to be pulling his eyeballs back into their sockets. I reached over without thinking and adjusted his hat back into place.

Finally his lips. He had to reach all the way around his head with both hands to bring his lips back to size. I grimaced as I thought about how he was going to do that. If he used the same approach as with his ears, ohhh, I cringed at the thought. But all he did was to gather his limp, elongated lips in his hands and, by remolding them, he was able to fix them properly. He puckered and grimaced a few times to make sure they were in working order. Then, pulling a mirror out of nowhere, he looked at the effect. "Perfect," he declared, planting a kiss on the mirror, which immediately vanished. With everything once again as it should be, he turned his attention back to me.

"Got you to smile, didn't I?" he teased. "Funny how a little smart remark can just set me off!" he exclaimed. "No offense," he tried to explain, "but when you asked 'What's so funny?' ...well... that was hysterical!"

Then he cleared his throat and simply stopped speaking. I figured it was my turn.

"I haven't laughed that hard in a long time," I admitted. "But I still don't know who you are. Or why you are here. Or why I am here. It's a relief to laugh for a change," I said, hoping he would take this as a compliment and go easy on me.

"Well, well, well," he commented, stroking his chin like a wise guy. "This is so much fun! I'm not sure if I should tell you who I am or- if I should make you guess...." And of course he laughed hysterically, knowing he had the advantage. I had never in my life seen someone having so much fun. Was it normal, I wondered, to be so spontaneous?

"I, of course, have a distinct advantage because I know you and all about you. And I have to say that you have been a most miserable person—possibly the most miserable I have ever encountered." He started giggling as he finished the last sentence. "I am so sorry," he said as he choked on his laughter. "But if you could only see yourself sometimes!" He gave up and fell on the ground laughing.

I watched him writhing, clutching his sides laughing at me. This felt like a pretty harsh judgment. I knew I wasn't the life of the party, but I wasn't that bad, was I? It probably did seem silly to some people that I was so serious, but hey, hadn't my hard work paid off? Don't answer that question, I told myself just as quickly.

He finally got hold of himself. "As you can see, I, myself, am undeniably joyous," he continued.

'And ridiculous' were the words I would have used to end his sentence, but I kept quiet.

"I hope that I do not offend you greatly." This last statement he made with as much compassion as a completely happy person can have, which was hardly enough to even begin to help me.

"No offense is taken by your joy," I explained, smiling helplessly at his effort to be serious. In spite of feeling offended by his judgment of me as the most miserable person he had ever met, I was intrigued. "I just do not understand it or what you have to teach me."

Chapter xxxi

What could I possibly learn from such a strange fellow? I told him what I was thinking, admitting that I didn't believe he was the right person—I mean spirit—for the job.

"How can I take anything you say seriously?" I asked. "Especially dressed as you are? And while I find your behavior comical and fun, the only thing I can gather is that you think I should lighten up. I do envy you your joy," I said honestly, "but isn't life supposed to be taken seriously, especially when one is trying to learn a new way of being, such as I am? What does all this have to do with me?"

There. That ought to deflate him a little bit.

"What does all this have to do with you?" he cried excitedly. "Oh, only everything!" he declared and off he went again into another round of wild antics, causing me to smile and then giggle, and then collapse in laughter again. It just felt so good. "I really should laugh more often," I told myself. I looked over at the candles sitting beside me. They were going wild.

Resuming a slightly more composed demeanor, he went on. "I will not keep you in suspense any longer, my friend. And it's really quite simple. I am your Spirit of Abundant Joy and Incredible Fun. No reason to envy me, is there?" he asked grinning at my surprised expression as he revealed himself.

"You can call me SAJIF," he added, putting the emphasis on the second syllable. "Also, while I do apologize for my appearance if it offends you," he said with aplomb, "I need to remind you that you're in charge of the costumes here, you know. I rather like the attire myself."

"Oh. Yes. Of course," I replied. I had forgotten that. "Is learning how to experience Abundant Joy and Incredible Fun my next lesson, SAJIF?" I asked.

"Oh, you are so smart!" he replied in harmless mockery. "Yes, alas, it is my duty to teach you about that," he admitted.

"What a shame that one has to be taught to recognize one's own spirit of joy and fun," he commented. "But after being a part of your life for so long, I know these are foreign concepts to you. Yes, this is your next lesson, if you are ready," and he grinned, compelling me to join in.

Chapter xxxii

"OK," I said somewhat dubiously. "But I still don't understand where you are going with this."

"Oh, my dear, dear woman." SAJIF danced merrily on his toes, hardly able to contain his excitement as he proceeded. "Abundant Joy and Incredible Fun are the very cornerstones of the true foundation of your life! It's about choosing to live from the place that makes your life authentic and real. It's where your greatness hides. It loves to play hide and seek, you see, and it's ready when you are. Your life is always so serious and hard, well... we've got some playing to do, is all I can say!

"When you live from where you think you *have to* live or do what you think you *have to do* with your life, that's where it gets all mucked up.

"Don't you see? That is where you have been stuck, and it hasn't been very joyful or much fun, has it? Don't you remember how deeply miserable you have been?" He finished and gasped for breath. He had been so excited to share this that he had hardly been able to breathe.

I remembered my misery. He didn't have to bring it up again.

"You asked for help, and that's what brought you here," he reminded me.

I had never considered joy and fun as necessities. "Can one be full of abundant joy and incredible fun without looking and acting ridiculous?" I asked, concerned that I might be asked to re-create myself to look like him or to act like him. I didn't think I could do that.

SAJIF laughed uproariously, spraying stardust all over as he turned somersaults and cartwheels merrily in front of me. "Oh sure you can, but it's very difficult!" he gasped breathlessly. "You really ought to try this sometime."

Then a bit more subdued, he added, "You can express joy however you want to, Avery Victoria Spencer... after all, it's your life!

"Please understand that I can hardly be expected to be calm and civilized right now. I am so glad to see you and to be talking with you! We haven't spent any time together, you and I. I can't remember the last time you gave me a thought or chose to spend any time with me. All this is almost too much. I am soooooo happy!" And with that, he fairly flew down the hall and back.

"I'm just releasing some years of pent-up joy. I'm sure I'll settle down eventually, although I hope not!" he added gaily.

I had to admit that he was right. I hadn't been much fun. Ever. People had teased me about that all my life. Joy, abundant or otherwise, hadn't occurred to me as I seriously pursued my goals. Let alone fun. Even in college, where I saw scores of young people having fun, I applied myself to my double majors so that I could make something of myself.

Make something of myself? As if my own self weren't good enough? It suddenly struck me how awful that sounded, even to me. I had been intent on making something up for my life, rather than ever considering how to express my true self. That must be where the abundant joy and incredible fun came in. Those feelings must be the doorway to my own real self, my greatness. That must be why my life had been so serious. And hard. And why my financial burdens felt so heavy. I hadn't considered either as relevant to my pursuit of a secure financial future.

"My dear, dear A.V.," SAJIF said kindly, reading my thoughts, "you are in a magical place. You can do whatever you imagine here. You can experience abundant joy and have incredible fun here. In fact, that's an order!" he commanded trying to look serious and authoritative. And then he started giggling, obviously impressed with his own wit.

He was testing my limits of endurance. No one called me "A.V." But SAJIF used it in such an endearing way, I let it go. Seeing how earnestly I was listening, he went on, "You need not go outside of yourself to find your own greatness, your own unique purpose, and your own special abundant joy and incredible fun in life. All of it is already inside you. Your entire life has been full of purpose up to this point. It has brought you to this place, hasn't it? You have just been too sad, miserable, and scared to see it, but each step you have taken is part of your journey to this great discovery. And some people never get this far. So you should be delighted!

"The question you must answer now is how to go on from here, expressing your purposeful greatness with abundant joy and incredible fun. The answer is within you, and it is easy to realize. Perhaps too easy for one who has believed that you must find it through misery, sacrifice, heaviness, hardship, and suffering. In quietness and confidence, with abundant joy and incredible fun, you will find what you seek."

Chapter xxxiii

"Down this corridor are many doors, representing the choices you have created for yourself in this lifetime," SAJIF continued.

"Right now, you may choose one, and only one, to enter. Only one leads to a life of abundant joy and incredible fun. Once you open one of the doors, you will not be able to enter any of the others. Or you may choose not to enter any of the doors and leave this place."

"But how do I know which one is the right one?" I whined. I hated making personal choices. I was great at big decisions for the bank, but for myself... I was afraid I'd make the wrong one. I was a great hesitator.

"Ah, my dear friend, that is the great paradox. While you can only choose one door, you cannot choose the wrong door. Do you understand? There are no mistakes here. Behind any door you choose is a meaningful life experience. But you cannot have them all, just one now or none at all. It is up to you. Isn't this *fun*?" SAJIF was so excited he wiggled and whirled as he chattered to me. "We should make this a TV game show!"

I did not share his enthusiasm. He had to know how hard that would be for me—to pick just one.

"I must leave you now, my dearest Avery. But it has brought me the greatest joy to spend this time with you. Just remember what I have told you."

SAJIF started to spin slowly, around and around. I remembered fondly the days of childhood when I would spin until I fell to the ground. Then I would stand up to walk, but the dizziness would overwhelm me, and I'd stagger around, laughing and disoriented. That seemed like lifetimes ago. Oh yes, I'd had a few moments of fun in my life. I remembered that now.

As my now-beloved Spirit of Abundant Joy and Incredible Fun spun ever faster and faster, he seemed to gain momentum until he was spinning so fast I could no longer recognize him. Then he seemed to evaporate in a glorious display of golden stardust. His exit was as dramatic and interesting as his entry had been.

As my fascination settled down, I realized that I was still in the hallway, alone, except for both candles which remained with me. The doors ahead seemed to beckon. There were so many to choose from, and yet he had told me I had to choose just one. I hesitated as I felt anxiety returning to me.

I deplored making personal decisions because when selecting one option, I immediately regretted all the other options I would not be able to choose. The truth was, I never trusted the decisions I did make. I almost always spent more time regretting the loss of the other choices than concentrating on the positive sides of the one I had made.

My frustration grew, and proportionately, so did the sense that I was leaving the hallway. The doors in front of me began to blur. I did not want to leave this place without making a decision. I knew that if I gave in to this feeling now, I would be back in my life with nothing resolved.

Recognizing that these anxious feelings could never guide me, I had to figure out a way to make them go away. Just in time I got a grip on the situation and cried out loud, "I choose!" I spoke with sincere feeling and great conviction. Immediately, the hallway came back into focus.

It was true that SAJIF had told me that I did not have to choose a door, that I could leave without choosing. But I had realized just in time that to do so would never be acceptable to me. I knew I would go into one of the rooms. I would not leave this place without that experience. Not to choose was unacceptable. I turned to gaze out the window as I contemplated my decision.

As I gazed out the window, I could see the same patio where I had sat with the Spirit of Greatness. I saw the harbor, the ships sailing out to sea. As I let myself enjoy this scene, and just breathe with delight at what was happening before me in this moment, it occurred to me that the same statement was true about my life in general. Not to choose was unacceptable. But the choice had to be made based on what brought me joy and a sense of fun, for there I would find the greatness that was playing this hide and seek game. It wanted me to look for it, right here in the middle of fun and joy. Certainly neither had not been the criteria for decisions about my life to this point.

The dilemmas I encountered in life were simply the result of my own fear of choosing, my own fear of making the wrong choice, my own fear of losing other opportunities. For too long, I had pursued a life that I felt would be prestigious and acceptable... and safe. But it hadn't worked that way. I wasn't safe. I was lonely, deeply in debt, and extremely vulnerable. Fear had gotten me where I was, and I was determined that it would not control my choices from this moment forward. I took a deep breath, closed my eyes, and became quiet. All I really needed to do was breathe and listen to my wisdom. I let myself glide into the blissful peace of the moment.

Chapter xxxiv

When I opened my eyes and looked again at the doors in front of me, instead of so many doors to chose from, now there was only one, and it was open.

Suddenly everything was so obvious, so clear. I did not have to analyze or guess at anything. I was letting my own wisdom make the choice, and I knew it was the only right one for me, for this moment. I also knew that this would apply not only to this choice, but also to all my future decisions. My spirit was giving me a glimpse of how to make 'right' choices. And SAJIF was right. There were no wrong choices, anyway. Each one I made would take me where I needed to go at the right time.

The corridor of too many doors had depicted the way I usually made decisions in my life. Just as if I were in such a hallway, I would consider all the choices I had. There were usually enough to overwhelm me with options. Then I would become so frustrated that I would either end up picking none of them or wait until my options eliminated themselves, leaving me totally dissatisfied and unhappy. Or I would pick one and then lament that I hadn't chosen another. How reluctant I had been to make a decision about my personal life! Over and over, I had preferred to let the 'decision make me.'

Now I knew that all I needed to do was to focus my attention, become quiet, and listen to my own wisdom. All I needed was within me: my own sense of things, my own spirit, my own greatness, my own sense of abundant joy and incredible fun.

Chapter xxxv

What lessons were in store for me behind this open door? What discoveries about myself would be revealed when I entered this room? It's amazing what a mind can imagine when walking into the unknown. Eternity lives in that moment.

The door seemed to be inviting me to enter. I peeked inside cautiously and noticed a fire crackling joyfully in the fireplace. I had to step all the way inside to see that it contained only a simple wooden table where a woman was seated, writing. Otherwise, the room was empty—no other furniture, adornment, or decoration.

I had hoped for something a little more elaborate. Then I had to laugh at myself. Of course the room was singular and explicit. Were it full of other life, other images, the message would not have been as clear and direct. This way, I could not mistake the interpretation of the message I saw before me.

The woman writing at the desk remained completely absorbed in her task. She did not register any acknowledgement that I had entered the room. I watched from a distance, not wanting to disturb her.

She sat facing a window at the back of the room, so that I could not see her face except as a vague reflection in the window glass. Her long, blazing-red hair fell forward providing a curtain of privacy as she sat intent upon her task. She was dressed in a beautiful mahogany-colored robe—simple, refined, and comfortable. The room almost sparkled with her aliveness and joyful sense of purpose. I ached to see what she was writing and cleared my throat to get her attention.

No response. The candle on her desk, now a familiar sight to me, burned steadily and delightfully. I remembered my own candle in the hallway and thought about retrieving it. But I did not want to break the spell of this moment.

As I walked toward the desk, the sound of the pen moving across the paper filled the otherwise silent room. What a beautiful sound it was, one I had marveled at when I would write occasional letters and stories as a child. How I had loved the feel of pen against paper! How I had loved words that formed themselves into stories!

Her book was leather-bound, full of fine paper. Her pen, simple, such as a medieval scribe might have used, and an ink well sat close at hand. Her handwriting was gloriously artistic, and I marveled at the beauty of the page as she filled it with words.

Words. They had been my first love from as far back as I could remember. I had taught myself to read even before I had begun school. Words distracted me from all other life events. I would rather be with words than anything I could think of.

How had I gotten into the world of numbers? And then I realized that numbers required nothing creative of me. They were what they were, safe. There were no choices with numbers. One plus one would always equal two. And so I had replaced my love of words with something that I felt was safe and certain.

I could not resist the desire to look over the woman's shoulder to read as she wrote. She, on the other hand, remained oblivious to my proximity. She was writing on the last page of the book, apparently at the end of her writing. This is what I read:

"I say to you this, that nothing outside of yourself can tell you the truth about yourself. And not only this, but every circumstance that you create outside of yourself is meant to draw you to your own soul. It is right to study, to learn, and to grow in knowledge, but only your own spirit can take that knowledge into itself and ignite it with the flame of its own truth.

"Do not seek to answer the questions of your spirit with mere facts and circumstances. Neither rely too heavily on the opinions of others. Seek instead to listen to the magic of what lies within you and move as it leads.

"Be mindful and intent upon that which expresses your own true greatness and sense of joy and fun lest you compare yourself with others, become distracted, and offend the unique greatness of your own self.

"It is not through loud voices clamoring for your attention that you will find the way, but through your own quiet spirit, which simply waits for your attention.

"It is not through resolute effort and force of will that you will find your purpose, but through the spirit of your own joy, the spirit that leads you toward that to which you long to give yourself, completely. And these discoveries are made as you express yourself—your wondrous, glorious, authentic self— however you choose to do that.

"Do not fret about the physical world and the obstacles you think you see. They are created by you for a purpose and are illusions through which your spirit guides your growth.

"The burden of your financial woes has been part of your lesson; it has served as a tool and should never be considered anything but a way to the truth you have desired to learn, from your own wisdom.

"The story of your journey lies within these pages. There is nothing you need to do, just live the truth contained herein and share it with the world."

As I read, the gentle truth of the words brought tears to my eyes. I found that the writer was gone, and I was in her place. This was my book, this message mine, and I was the author.

The last instruction appeared before my eyes, yet I did not pick up a pen to write it down.

"This book is about you, but not only about you. Share it with others so that they, too, may see that the only way to true fulfillment and purpose is by listening to and honoring their own inner wisdom.

"Let that which is within you come forth. Let your light shine brilliantly."

What of the doors I had not opened? I smiled to myself. Full of the joy of heartfelt purpose, I was utterly convinced that behind each one, I would have found this singular vision. I saw that I had created the illusion of many doors to keep myself from knowing the wonder of this glorious moment—the moment when I realized that I was a special person, full of wisdom, grace, courage, and greatness. I felt that my overwhelming financial burden had been lifted and that my money issues were resolved. I was suddenly profoundly grateful for what my debts had taught me. I knew now, as I never had known before, that I had been delivered. This journey was not about the money. It was far more important than that.

I closed the book, and, as I lifted it from the desk, I awoke.

Epilogue

By the Author

It is now some time since the writing of this first volume. I began to understand experientially what I had learned from my inner wisdom. The burden of financial woe that I carried began to melt away in amazing and unexpected ways. Over the course of a relatively short period of time, so did the outward manifestation—my immense debt load.

The funny thing is that my debts became my teachers, and, in a way, my friends. My perspective of them changed entirely. I was grateful for the lessons they taught me, and they no longer felt like burdens, but rather, gifts. I realized that they had been a way to draw me into my own wisdom. Truly, as I focused more on what was inside of me that expressed my greatness, brought me abundant joy and even surprised me as the experience of 'fun,' my issues with money faded away, like an early morning mist.

I learned that my own way of perceiving any decision I should make or the direction to follow in relation to any financial decision was to simply become quiet and sense the feeling of 'heaviness' or 'lightness' I experienced. Where did my spirit, my wisdom, want to go? As I gave my innermost self permission to guide me, my sense of direction became clear and my burden of financial woe lifted. As a result, I became acutely sensitive to choices that seemed burdensome or weighty and recognized this as my own personal 'guidance system.'

Whatever changes I made to my life felt liberating. Interestingly, I would not consider that I made any dramatically complicated or 'hard' external changes to my life, just simple ones, directed from within. I stepped away from some relationships and activities that I had not enjoyed. When I became frustrated, I began to listen to what was going on inside rather than going on a shopping spree. Somehow, I found I was making better decisions and had a keener sense of judgment, but at the same time, I was content and perhaps a bit more 'my self.'

As I have become more of 'who I really am,' my relationship with money has become more genuine. I no longer try to keep up or prove anything. What a relief that is! What I choose to use my money for now reflects the deepest desires of my heart.

I still love to surround myself with beauty, but beauty no longer means clutter and excess. Beauty has become more simple, more spacious, more peaceful. I manage my money in a way that blesses both the present and the future.

You may wonder whether this journey was real. Of course not, in any physical sense. But where it really matters, on the emotional, soulful level of life, it has transformed me. That is what is real, and the results are very real.

This journey happened in my heart. I traveled deep into the recesses of my soul to discover this amazing place that I believe exists in every person. It is there that I discovered the wisdom that changed the course of my relationship with money, and not only with money, but also my perspective of my life.

With all this bliss, I expected to float in ecstasy through the rest of my life. Like the Apostle Paul's one-time and complete conversion on the road to Damascus, I expected to pack up the aura of my experience in the castle and never encounter another burdensome experience... ever. As if a divine halo sat on my head. I was just a little disappointed to learn that my salvation was not complete, that it would come in steps, as it does for most of us.

It seems to me in retrospect that the immensity of the burden of financial woes had so overwhelmed me that I had not realized that I carried others. But I did. I was to learn that my life would be a series of 'wisdoms' learned from burdens I carried. Each one would take me to a deeper level of understanding. And I came to see they were not really burdens, but precious gifts; each one to guide me into greater wisdom, and a richer, more authentic life.

But I am getting ahead of myself, for there are other stories to follow.

Ruth Theobald Probst
November 2003

Coming in 2005

Watch for Volume II,
in which Avery
ventures farther on her journey.

Avery Victoria Spencer

Acknowledgements

How does one thank everyone who helps to create a book? Or any art form for that matter? Just as 'no man is an island,' no book comes into being without the most determined support, wise counsel, and serendipitous encounters.

This book journey has been full of such wondrous events for which I am profoundly thankful. As a first-time author, there are any number of times I would have been happy to tuck this story away and forget about bringing it to print. Thankfully, others thought differently. And perhaps something beyond my own ego agreed.

First, I recognize the great wisdom of the universe that came to me one night and brought me a dream from which not only this story began, but also my own issues with money began to heal. Let's just acknowledge the fact that stories come from a source beyond our known world. Authors get credit for their great imaginations, often the true Source does not receive any recognition.

The first overriding influence to publish this fable comes from my shameful dread of meeting my deceased mother in the next life if I do not. Her life, the difficulties she faced, the burdens she carried to the end, inspired me to seek the wisdom of my own burdens, to learn the message of these incredible gifts in this lifetime. She has inspired me to that purpose.

I believe many books are never born. Conceived, yes, but 'miscarried' by adverse influences. Those closest to the author can kill the spirit of the work before it has a chance to breathe. Books must be protected and ideas nourished while they develop in the soul of the author.

This book would never have come to life if my beloved husband, Thomas Probst, had in any way suggested, inferred, hinted, thought, or transmitted through his psychic aura that the book was a bad idea. A mere breath of hesitation could have had stopped the fledgling heartbeat. From the serendipitous encounter in 1985 that drew us to each other, he has supported me always. During the writing process he has respected my time to write, listening as I have read sections of the story aloud to him, encouraging me to be the best I can be... to be who I really am. Always, ever, he has my love.

What does a first-time author do with a book? Especially if she is a reluctant author? If she's smart, she hires Ellen Reid's "Smarketing" group to surround herself with people who know

how to encourage its development. I 'happened' to read Dan
Poynter's book, *The Self-Publishing Manual* and met Ellen
through the book's 'Resource' section. Ellen's candor,
enthusiasm, creativity, honesty, and willingness to listen to me
whine endlessly during the months of labor to bring this story
to publication, gave birth to this book. She has been the patient,
loving midwife. I am convinced this book would not have been
published without her dedication and encouragement. Period.

Through Ellen I met Laren Bright, who created the back
cover and inside flap text. Ellen read his writing to me over the
phone as I sat in the Dallas airport one afternoon and I wept at
the way he captured the essence of the story. Laren also did
some timely conceptual edits after I expanded the story based on
a trip inspired by my husband to parts of Austria and Germany.
Laren, you are a gift and truly your light has shined 'brightly.'

Also through Ellen, I met Dotti Albertine. Her creativity
made the book cover glow with the spirit of the story in a way
I could not have envisioned.

Some books have one primary editor. This one has had
several whose combined efforts have enriched its content. I
'happened' to meet the first editor of the story, Barbara Passero,
while we were waiting in the cold Boston wind for a shuttle to
pick us up at the airport. Her critical talent, offered kindly and
supportively, gave me hope in the early days of the publication

process. She has continued to review my new materials. I know we met for a purpose.

To my critical grammatical editor, Andrea Howe, who swiftly brought the laborious process of editing to a close, you are incredible. I could never do what you do, and I am so glad you do!

Melissa Reischman, thank you for making the 'coat of arms' symbol for the Avery Victory Spencer book series come to life. All you had to work with was an idea in my head, and you knew just what to do.

To the staff of Goblin Fern Press who took the book from its edited version into production, fine tuning each page, finding the best printer, and setting up the marketing program for the book, my thanks. Kira Henschel, Drew Burns, as I have journeyed around the country doing my work, I have rested easy, knowing you were caring for the final steps of the publication process. The fact that I 'found' you because my husband and I were shopping for furniture in a small store in the north woods of Wisconsin and happened to run into Kathleen Marsh, also a writer who had used your services, confirms once again, that this story was meant to be published.

To my staff at TheoPRO Compliance & Consulting, Inc., how can I ever thank you for going with me on this journey, which you know took time away from the other work we were doing. You have carried on, covered the bases, kept the company growing, and always supported me.

Pamela Leshok, my executive assistant, you came into my life at precisely the right time (imagine that!) and were the 'wind beneath my wings' to make critical decisions during the last days and weeks before publication.

Looking back, it's easy to see the significant moments in life and the people who inspire transformation. I would like to acknowledge those special people who helped me become who I am today: The staff of The Women's Center of Waukesha, Wisconsin, who in 1980 gave an emotionally bruised and physically undone woman the tools she needed to create a new life. To this day, I bless and support this organization for the work they are doing to help women literally re-create themselves into who they really are meant to be.

To my therapists, Joyce Wallskog, PhD, and during your battle with breast cancer, to Linda Stone, MSW; the journey out of a life history, in fact, a family history of depression and anxiety has been enabled by your dedication to my healing.

To my best friend on earth, Susan Losinske, everyone should be as fortunate as I to have a friend like you; someone to laugh and cry with, someone to care, encourage, and inspire while always gently telling the truth.

To my extended family, Hank and Pam Probst and my step-grandson Jacob (and his brother- or sister-to-be), Chuck and Juanita Probst, and Alyssa Probst, we have become a family together and I am blessed to have you in my life.

To Maria Tiegs, and beloved grandchildren Spencer, Avery, and Peyton, thank you for coming into my life. My son, Jonathan, has chosen his life mate well. I count you as a special and wonderful addition to my life.

Finally, to my own children, Sonia and Jonathan Tiegs, to whom I gave birth and who have journeyed with me through a rather eventful and often tumultuous life, I do not know how you have endured the ups and downs. Not only have you endured, but you have also created courageous and well-lived lives. I am the luckiest mother alive to have your love. Please know that no matter what, my heart reaches to yours each and every day.

For information on other works by
Ruth Theobald Probst, or her workshops,
book signing and speaking events, or to invite
her to speak to your group, please visit her website:
www.wisdomofourburdens.com